GRAN TURISMO™ 4
THE REAL DRIVING SIMULATOR

DRIVING THE GAME

GRAN TURISMO™ 4
THE REAL DRIVING SIMULATOR

DRIVING THE GAME

LEO HARTAS

ILEX

First published in the United Kingdom in 2005 by:

I L E X
3 St Andrews Place
Lewes
East Sussex
BN7 1UP
www.ilex-press.com

This book was conceived by Jason Fitzgerald
(Product Manager: Gran Turismo, Sony Computer Entertainment
Europe) and designed and produced by ILEX:
THE ILEX PRESS Ltd
Cambridge
England

Publisher: Alastair Campbell
Executive Publisher: Sophie Collins
Creative Director: Peter Bridgewater
Senior Project Editor: Steve Luck
Design Manager: Tony Seddon
Designer: Jonathan Raimes

British Library Cataloguing-in-Publication Data
A catalogue record for this book is available
from the British Library

ISBN 1-904705-55-3

Printed and bound by Butler and Tanner

www.granturismoworld.com

CONTENTS

GRAN TURISMO™ 4
THE REAL DRIVING SIMULATOR

DRIVING THE GAME

06

MOST OF US DON'T GET THE OPPORTUNITY TO EXPERIENCE THE THRILL OF 200 BHP BURSTING FROM THE STARTING GRID IN AN EAR-SPLITTING ROAR. WE CAN ONLY DREAM OF TEARING INTO THE FIRST BEND, POWER-SLIDING, RIPPING INTO THE STRAIGHT, TAKING THE LEAD, PUSHING THE LIMITS OF DRIVER AND MACHINE.

SINCE GRAN TURISMO WAS FIRST RELEASED IN JAPAN IN 1997 THE SERIES HAS GONE TO SELL OVER 36 MILLION UNITS MAKING IT ONE OF THE THE BEST-SELLING VIDEO GAMES EVER.

1. A 2003 Nissan 350Z driving the notoriously testing Nürburgring circuit in Germany.
2. The 2004 PlayStation Pescarolo C60 LMP Judd on the streets of Paris.

08

1

On the race tracks of the world the line between reality and digital is blurring. Apart from the physical sensations of movement, smell and the risk of injury, the simulation is almost complete, brought to life in the etched silicon of a PlayStation 2 console. This alternate reality is called Gran Turismo.

Gran Turismo is a digital recreation of the driving world, and one that is so accurate that the game is itself feeding back into reality. The Gran Turismo 4 game engine can now be found testing the behaviour of prototype cars before the model goes into full manufacture. Gran Turismo's world is accurate to within 99%. This isn't a hollow marketing claim, circuits have been time trialled by professional race drivers driving the same cars both in the real world and in GT4 and in terms of differential in lap times there was a hair's breadth between them.

Gran Turismo fulfils the dream of every armchair racer. Knowing the car you have chosen to race is as close a replica as possible to the real thing, from bhp to the sound of the engine, gives a thrill only driving the real thing can match.

Players can pit their driving skills against those of the professionals on the same circuits and in the same cars. And what a line up of cars; in GT4 the player is treated to over 650 vehicles, from the very birth of motoring to the latest technology-laden super-cars.

Gran Turismo 4 has also introduced Photo mode. At first glance it looks like an adjunct to the real business taking place on the circuits and tracks, but instead it graphically displays the level of visual realism GT4 has achieved. Photo mode allows the player to reflect on the rich variety and sometimes beauty of the most influential machines of the modern age.

With adrenalin pumping as you scream at 200 kph into the tortuous Karussell bend at Nürburgring, Europe's most gruelling test circuit, there isn't much time to think about anything except the brakes. In the game, that is how it should be, but there is so much missed as the landscape zips by. This book momentarily stops time to give you a chance to marvel at the amazing work of automotive art that is Gran Turismo.

CAR MAKERS NOW SEE GT AS A SERIOUS MARKETING
OPPORTUNITY THAT CAN'T BE MISSED. OVER 80 CAR
COMPANIES NOW CONTRIBUTE TO THE TITLE INCLUDING
MANY HOUSEHOLD NAMES.

1. Mitsubishi Lancer Evolution VIII MR, the real thing at a Polyphony test day.

2

4

3

5

2. A Lancia Delta HF Integrale WRC Group A rally car, enjoying the sights of the Grand Canyon.

3. The Mercedes SL55 AMG could reach 0–60 mph in a staggering 4.6 seconds.

4. The Mazda MX-5 with its good looks and sporty performance became an instant best seller.

5. It's not just the best of modern cars that feature in GT. The Honda N360 first went into production in 1967.

01 OVERTAKE
THE HISTORY OF GRAN TURISMO

010

JUST SEVEN SHORT YEARS AGO THE ORIGINAL GRAN TURISMO WAS RELEASED ON PLAYSTATION 1 —AND IT WAS A CASE OF LEADING RIGHT FROM THE VERY START. IN THAT SHORT TIME THE GAME HAS SEEN THREE DIFFERENT VERSIONS AND MASSIVE LEAPS OF TECHNICAL EXCELLENCE BOTH IN HARDWARE—THE JUMP TO PS2 —AND THE SOFTWARE ITSELF.

GRAN TURISMO WAS NAMED AFTER THE TRANSPORT—THE HORSES AND CARRIAGES—USED BY ROMANTIC TRAVELERS IN THE 17TH AND 18TH CENTURIES WHO CROSSED EUROPE ON THE GRAND TOUR—A JOURNEY OF CLASSICAL DISCOVERY.

The 2000 TVR Tuscan Speed 6 climbing the streets of Citta di Aria, Assisi, Italy.

01 OVERTAKE
THE DRIVING-GAME GENRE

012

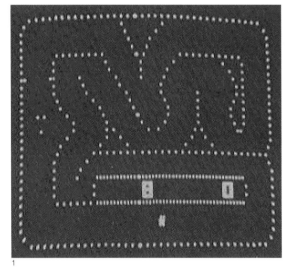

1

YOUR SCORE 061   TOP SPEED 174

GEAR 4   EXPERT

2

Nolan Bushnell, the founder of Atari, realized the potential of a driving game in 1971, but it wasn't until 1974 that the world saw the first arcade game in Gran Trak 10. From this point on, although the market grew in all directions, it was Atari that often made the significant technical advances. Two years after the release of Gran Trak 10, Atari released Sprint 2 and proved that the driving-game genre could be a commercial success. While good fun to play, these early examples featured a simple overhead view that was far from the experience of real driving.

In 1976 Atari released Night Driver, the first first-person driving game and the first to nod in the direction of realism. The game used a system of scaling 2D sprites to simulate a 3D environment, an approach that became more sophisticated in games such as Turbo by Sega in 1981.

Perhaps the greatest milestone in this period of the genre's history was Pole Position by Namco which, although brought out in 1982, was still to be found in arcades a decade later. The game was important because it was the first game to simulate the real racing experience, and even though the graphics look crude by today's standards, they were revolutionary at the time. It was also the first game to be based on a real track (Fuji). The notion of realism was limited in that all of these games, until the advent of affordable home computers and consoles, were played on coin-operated machines that only supported short, arcade-style play.

Real-time vector-based 3D, the same display principle that GT uses, first arrived in 1977 in the form of Speed Freaks by Vectorbeam. Although using genuine 3D, Speed Freaks could only display white line "wireframes" of the cars and tracks on a

DESPITE FINDING ITSELF IN ONE OF THE MOST COMPETITIVE
OF ALL GAME GENRES, GRAN TURISMO'S ATTENTION TO DETAIL
SETS IT APART FROM THE OTHERS.

1. Gran Trak 10 (1974), Atari. From the very beginning, driving perfectly suited the computer game.

2. Night Driver (1976), Atari. A first-person view based on a system of scaling 2D sprites.

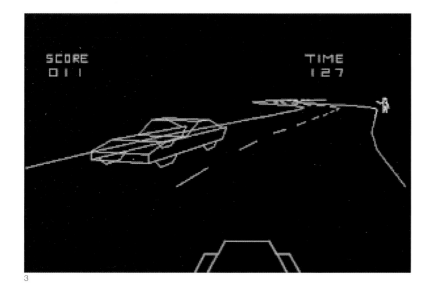

3

black background. Perhaps the most interesting game that pointed toward the graphics and physics realism of GT was another Atari game, Hard Drivin', released in 1989. Although knockabout fun in game play (drivers had to complete loop-the-loops) the game used a realistic physics engine and was the first driving simulator to use filled polygons.

Ridge Racer by Namco was launched in 1993 and came to dominate car driving both at the arcades and on PlayStation. The game defined a new level of graphics realism based on textured polygons. However, the first game to use actual photographs to texture cars, tracks, and landscapes, Crusin' USA, was released a year later by Midway.

At present the driving-game genre sports a wide spectrum of both game play and style on every platform, from cartoon knockabout such as EA's Cel Damage to the detailed realism of Codemasters' ToCA Race Driver. With the increasing capacity of modern hardware, new sub-genres have sprung up such as the driving adventure, where the player is no longer tied to a track, but has the freedom of the city, as in Sony's Getaway and Rockstar's Grand Theft Auto.

At the centre of the genre remains the pursuit of the most realistic driving experience. Gran Turismo finds itself in a crowded and highly competitive market, but has, from the very outset, been the benchmark by which other games are measured.

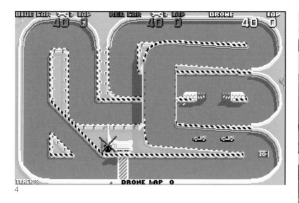

4

5

6

3. Speed Freaks (1977), Vectorbeam. The first example of a real-time vector-based 3D game.

4. Super Sprint (1986), Atari. The top down driving game revisited, with numerous visual enhancements.

5-6. Motor Toon Grand Prix (1996), Sony Computer Entertainment. Kazunori's precursor to the Gran Turismo series.

THE DRIVING FORCE

KAZUNORI YAMAUCHI

014

THE LATEST COMPUTER GAMES ARE MASSIVE UNDERTAKINGS, AND GRAN TURISMO IS NO EXCEPTION. IT EMPLOYS A TEAM OF AROUND 60-70, CONTRIBUTING THOUSANDS OF MAN-HOURS. THEY ARE INSPIRED BY THE CREATIVE VISION OF KAZUNORI YAMAUCHI.

As a schoolboy in Kashiwa, Japan, Kazunori initially looked to a career in the movies, even establishing a movie-production company and making a film every year. At university he concentrated on graphic design, sometimes working part-time preparing presentations for car manufacturers.

Kazunori joined Sony Music, Japan in 1992, and a year later moved to the new division of Sony Computer Entertainment Inc., where he worked on the Motor Toon Grand Prix series. It was during this time, four years ahead of the first Gran Turismo game, that Kazunori conceived the idea of creating the ultimate racing simulator.

In 1996 he transferred to SCEI's Yoshida team, where he began work on the first GT, combining many elements from existing championship games, such as Le Mans 24 Hours and Formula 1, to create the most comprehensive driving game on any games platform.

AS A CHILD OF THREE, KAZUNORI WAS TAKEN BY HIS FATHER ON BUSINESS TRIPS IN AN ORIGINAL NISSAN SKYLINE. FROM THIS EARLY AGE HE DEVELOPED AN AFFINITY WITH THE MACHINE AROUND HIM, BOTH ITS KINETIC FUNCTION AND AS A MASTERPIECE OF INDUSTRIAL DESIGN.

1

3

2

1. Kazunori is an accomplished driver in his own right with an almost unequaled experience of a wide variety of cars.

2. Kazunori at his desk at Polyphony.

3. Here Kazunori explains his vision for the intro movie to a helicopter pilot at the Nürburgring.

4

December 1997 saw the release in Japan of Gran Turismo to wide critical acclaim. By the end of 1998, just seven months after its global release, the game had sold 6.2 million units, making it one of the best-selling video games ever.

Kazunori left SCEI in April 1998 to set up Polyphony Digital, the dedicated development house that would continue the GT franchise, albeit in close partnership with Sony Computer Entertainment.

Throughout the development of GT and its sequels, Kazunori has been able to indulge his love of cars with the opportunity to test-drive them himself. Such is the breadth of his experience that many of the manufacturers themselves are eager for him to assess their prototypes.

Kazunori's own car collection changes regularly but has included an Alpine A10, Nissan 350L, Mercedes AMG 600SL, Ford GT, and a Mitsubishi Evo VII.

One of the most interesting elements of Kazunori's vision for GT is his understanding of the link between mathematical perfection and the visual arts. He strives tirelessly for realism in the game, but is equally keen to emphasize the visual beauty that it can generate. He understands that the complete driving experience is more than building an accurate driving simulator. It is the combination of every detail, from the shifting weight of the driver as the car turns, to the reflection of a sunset in a particular paint finish. Photo Mode, in GT4, is a celebration of this idea, freezing the frantic race to contemplate what an incredible visual masterpiece Polyphony has created.

5

6

4. Studying vehicle performance data.

5-6. The result of Kazunori's dream. Unparalleled driving simulation and a virtual graphics environment that rivals reality itself.

5. Kokusai Forum. Photo Mode.

6. Ice race GT4 in-game.

KAZUNORI DESCRIBES WHAT HE WANTED FROM THE TRACKS:
"WE ARE LOOKING FOR AS MUCH REALISM AS POSSIBLE
IN THE PHYSICS. WE DISCOVERED EACH LOCATION HAS A
DIFFERENT SURFACE; EVEN STANDARD ASPHALT CAN VARY
FROM TRACK TO TRACK."

OVERTAKE 01

GRAN TURISMO
HOW IT ALL BEGAN

019

FROM THE MOMENT IT WAS RELEASED IN DECEMBER 1997, GRAN TURISMO TOOK THE GAMING WORLD BY STORM. THE GAME WAS REVOLUTIONARY IN THE WAY IT RAISED THE STANDARD IN THE DRIVING GENRE TO UNTHINKABLE NEW LEVELS. GT FEATURED A DETAILED PHYSICS ENGINE, THE REALISM OF WHICH HADN'T BEEN SEEN BEFORE ON SONY'S PLAYSTATION 1.

The Toyota Tourer V MkII, Racing Modified Edition, in action.

GT'S ADVANCED HANDLING DEMONSTRATED PERFECTLY THE RECENTLY RELEASED DUALSHOCK GAME CONTROLLER, WHICH ALLOWED PRECISION ANALOGUE STEERING, AS WELL AS VIBRATION FEEDBACK.

01 OVERTAKE

GT1

020

Gran Turismo 1 established a successful game-design formula that has remained at the core all the way through subsequent versions. Aware that driving simulations needed to cater for two moods of game play, GT was designed with two driving modes—an arcade mode and a Gran Turismo mode. The arcade mode combined more forgiving handling physics with pick-up-and-play instant races and various multiplayer options. It resulted in an experience that any casual gamer would expect from a driving game.

The Gran Turismo mode, on the other hand, presented the real power behind the game, with a massive array of race events, each finely tuned to provide ever tougher challenges. It also featured the ability to win money, which could then be used to buy new cars or upgrades to existing ones—a subtle but effective way to progress through the game. For the real motoring devotees a system of licenses was introduced to improve the player's advanced driving skills and unlock new races.

IN MANY RESPECTS GRAN TURISMO 1 WAS AHEAD OF ITS TIME; THE FACT THAT ITS GAME-DESIGN FORMULA IS STILL AT THE HEART OF THE MORE RECENT VERSIONS OF THE GAME BEARS TESTAMENT TO THE THOUGHT BEHIND THE ORIGINAL GT.

1. Mitsubishi's powerful Lancer Evolution rally car shown in all the graphic detail of GT4.

2. Behind the steering wheel in GT1.

3. From the very beginning GT was all about racing virtual versions of real cars.

4. Even with the graphical limitations of the PS1 platform, the GT cars were as close as possible to the real originals.

5. Play selection options.

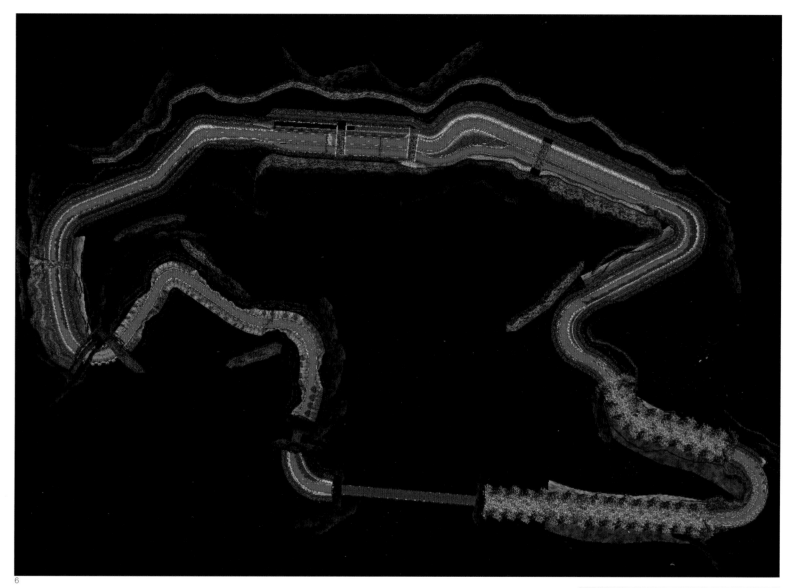

6

7

6-7. Trial mountain. Tracks, although fictional, were designed carefully to challenge the player without making it impossible to win.

1. The Nissan Skyline GT-R as featured in GT4.

GT2

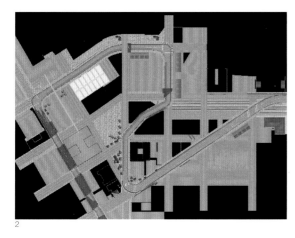

023

GT1 had established one of the biggest gaming franchises in the industry. Popular not only with players but also with car manufacturers, who were fast realizing the marketing power of including their products in the game, it was the first time big established businesses took video games seriously. This resulted in a leap from less than 10 car manufacturers working with Polyphony on GT1 to over 30 for the sequel. The team assembled 600 virtual vehicles on the grid, a world record for any single computer game.

GT2 was a huge game. It was so big, in fact, that its European release was on two discs: one for the arcade mode, the other for the Gran Turismo mode—which came as a novelty, race-track-scented, scratch-'n'-sniff disc. Along with the cars, every other area of GT was also expanded. Included in the 30

tracks there were now real-world tracks and exciting city-based circuits along with six off-road rally tracks which proved to be an instant hit. In taking players off-road, GT proved it could provide the fully comprehensive racing-game experience.

A new series of licenses were included, and a system that allowed players to transfer licenses gained on GT1 to the new game via a memory card. With the increase in cars came an even bigger increase in potentially available car parts—from engine blocks to hub caps. With the new tracks and the massive array of possible race events there was a danger that players could become lost in the variety of options. Polyphony catered for this by allowing players to track their progress, from unlocking one secret track or race event to the next, through a "percentage complete" screen.

2. City tracks debuted in GT3 to provide a new and exciting race environment.

3. The NSX-R Concept LM Race Car in action in GT4.

4. A Mazda Atenza in GT2. Notice not only the attention to detail on the car, but also the richness and realism of the background.

GRAPHICALLY GT2 IMPROVED ONLY SLIGHTLY ON THE ORIGINAL —MAINLY BECAUSE GT1 WAS ALREADY PUSHING AT PS1'S PROCESSING LIMITS. GT2, HOWEVER, SHOWED HOW TO SCALE UP AND EXPAND THE SHEER CONTENT VALUE THAT A RACING GAME COULD INCLUDE WHILE STILL RETAINING ITS TECHNICAL LEAD IN 32-BIT GAMING.

01 OVERTAKE
GT3

024

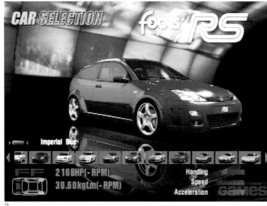

Originally Gran Turismo 3: A-Spec was expected to be a flagship product to herald the Japanese launch of PlayStation 2. However, the game arrived in Europe six months after the release of PS2, in the summer of 2001. There was a lot of anticipation about what Polyphony would do with the greater processing speed, storage capacity, and graphic capabilities that the new console offered.

GT3: A-Spec surpassed expectations. The immediate impressions were dominated by the spectacular rise in graphical realism with real-time reflections on the vehicles, sun-glare, and particle effects that created realistic dust, snow, and rain. After delving deeper into the game, players experienced a new physics engine that reproduced car handling with unprecedented realism. The AI (artificial intelligence) was also improved, making competing computer-controlled drivers more responsive, aggressive and unpredictable.

Following the success of GT3, Polyphony released GT Concept 2002 Tokyo–Geneva, which used the same game engine to create a lighter, more accessible game than GT3—one that offered 30 or so hours of play compared with GT3's 100 plus. Polyphony was able to track the evolution and development of cars by featuring around 80 models including early concepts, fantasy cars, and specialized rally cars.

WITH A STUNNING INCREASE IN THE REALISM OF ITS GRAPHICS, COMBINED WITH AN ENTIRELY NEW PHYSICS ENGINE, GT3 TOOK THE GAMING WORLD BY STORM.

1. The Peugeot 205 T16. GT3 A-Spec marketing material underlined the game's combination of the thrill of the race with the technical accuracy of the game.

2. A Ford Focus RS as the camera pans round the car at the race start countdown.

3. Car selection. Notice the use of manufacturers' correct logos.

4. A perfect GT season. The huge variety of challenges made for great longevity of play.

The GT3 experience:
5. Mitsubishi Lancer Evolution VII.
6. Mitsubishi Lancer Evolution WR1 Prototype.
7. Nissan Concept Z.
8. Nissan Skyline GT-R.
9. Mitsubishi Evolution VII.
10. Suzuki GSX-R/4 Concept.
11. Honda NSX.
12. Mitsubishi Evolution VII.
13. Nissan Skyline GT-R and Mazda RX-7.
14. Nissan Skyline GT-R Concept.

FAST CARS #1

PEUGEOT 205

THE PEUGEOT 205 SAW SUCCESS AS A RELIABLE AND FUEL-EFFICIENT SMALL CAR. IT ALSO FOUND SUCCESS ON THE RALLY TRACK AND STILL COMPETES TODAY.

026

VITAL STATISTICS: PEUGEOT 205

MAX POWER:	200 bhp @ 6750 rpm	**LENGTH:**	3.82 m	**ENGINE TYPE:**	1.8 litre/DOHC
MAX TORQUE:	255 Nm @ 4000 rpm	**TOTAL WIDTH:**	1.67 m	**ASPIRATION TYPE:**	Turbo
DISPLACEMENT: 1775 cc		**WHEEL BASE:**	2.54 m	**POWER/WEIGHT RATIO:**	0.17 bhp/kg
WEIGHT:	910 kg	**TREAD (FRONT):** 1.38 m		**TORQUE/WEIGHT RATIO:**	0.28 Nm/kg
HEIGHT:	1.41 m	**TREAD (REAR):**	1.33 m	**ARCADE MODE:**	YES

The Peugeot company released its first vehicle, a penny-farthing bicycle, in 1882. Although the company continued to produce bicycles (and still does), in 1889 Armand Peugeot presented a steam-driven three-wheel car at the World Fair. A year later the company had switched to

petrol and in 1929 the trademark model-naming (featuring an "0" in the middle) was introduced with the launch of the Peugeot 201.

The 205 was introduced in 1983 with a GT version released the following year. Available as both petrol and diesel, the car was a great success around the world. The specialized rally 205 Turbo 16, of which only 200 were built, appeared in the now defunct Group B rally in 1984, with a stunning victory at the Tour de Corse. Although almost uncontrollably powerful it went on to dominate Group B throughout 1985.

Despite the 205 ending production in 1999, with over 5 million sold, the car continues to rally both in national events worldwide and its own specific challenges. Its low cost and excellent performance make it an ideal choice for novice and amateur rally drivers.

02 GRID
PLANNING

028

THE MODERN ARTIFACT OF THE VIDEO GAME HAS BECOME A HUGE CONSTRUCT THAT RIVALS ANY HOLLYWOOD PRODUCTION. GONE ARE THE COTTAGE INDUSTRIES THAT CHARACTERIZED GAME DEVELOPMENT IN THE 1980s. TODAY'S GAMES REQUIRE THE COLLABORATION OF VARIED SPECIALIZATIONS AND DISCIPLINES THROUGH COMPLEX LAYERS OF DEVELOPMENT.

THE VIDEO GAME IS NO LONGER THE REALM OF SCHOOLBOY PROGRAMMERS, SOME OF WHOM BECAME MILLIONAIRES IN THE 1980s. THE VIDEO GAMES INDUSTRY IS NOW BIG BUSINESS, WITH THE DEVELOPMENT COSTS OF A FEW GAMES EXCEEDING THE BUDGETS OF MANY HOLLYWOOD MOVIES.

The Peugeot 205 Turbo 16 Evolution 2 Group B rally car was first seen in 1986.

02 GRID

THE GT SERIES
ACCELERATED EVOLUTION

030

"I AM VERY INVOLVED, DOWN TO THE DETAILS. EVEN TODAY I TAKE CARE OF THE GAME SYSTEM DESIGNS AND THE OVERALL ART DIRECTION FOR THE GT SERIES. I AM ALSO 'HANDS-ON' AND DIRECT ISSUES REGARDING THE CAR PHYSICS, USER INTERFACE DESIGNS, DEVELOPMENT METHODS, AND QUALITY OF CARS, TRACKS, AND REPLAY CAMERAS."
KAZUNORI YAMAUCHI

1. A view from the driving seat on the beautifully created Italian track.

KAZUNORI'S CONSTANT STRIVING FOR PERFECTION IN TERMS OF BOTH THE CARS' HANDLING AND THE CIRCUITS' VISUAL REALISM IS NOT ACHIEVED LIGHTLY.

The first Gran Turismo took six years to develop and was released in December 1997. GT2 took two years, and was released in December 1999. GT3 took a further three years, and was released in April 2001. Development on GT4 started in January 2001 and was to last three and a half years.

Kazunori describes his general thought process at pre-production like this: "When we created GT3 we were able to show nearly all of the advancements to the hardware platform PS2. This time around improvements to all areas has been the objective of the evolution: reviewing and improving development methods and skills, and the game system design as well. We generally don't make estimations on overall development timeframes." Beyond this, planning has to be flexible because GT4, like the previous titles and typical of almost all software development, was so reliant on research and development.

The development schedule was divided roughly into three stages, consuming a year each:

Stage One
Collect information and material.

Stage Two
Research and development, trial and error.

Stage Three
Development of title.

3

2

2. A Pontiac Vibe GTT in Las Vegas. Close-up perfection.

3. The TVR Speed 6 pictured here in atmospheric, black and white Photo Mode.

4. A PlayStation Pescarolo C60 LMP Judd racing through Paris.

4

BEHIND THE SCENES
LIFE OUTSIDE THE BOX

033

A CURSORY WALK AROUND THE POLYPHONY COMPLEX WOULD HAVE YOU THINKING OF IT LESS AS A PLACE OF WORK, AND MORE AS A COMPLETE, SELF-CONTAINED LIVING ENVIRONMENT, ALBEIT A GAMER'S VERSION OF ONE. ALONG WITH THE RANKS OF SIT-DOWN PS2 DRIVING CABINETS, YOU FIND RUNNING MACHINES, WEIGHTS, DRINKS MACHINES, AND POOL TABLES.

2

1. The President's office. His door is always open.

2. Polyphony's 60 or so employees often work 12 or more hours a day. The routine isn't strict: staff choose themselves when to start and finish, sometimes working through the night if they prefer.

POLYPHONY'S DIGITAL ETHOS:
"THERE ARE TWO WHEELS WHICH DRIVE POLYPHONY DIGITAL INC.—TECHNOLOGY AND DESIGN."

1

034

When hiring staff, Kazunori looks for a special kind of person: "I recruit staff whom I have met in various places, and look for people who will blend with the styles of Polyphony. The characteristics I would look for would be someone who is inquisitive of discoveries in technology, those who are very artistic, and those who are fair and honest."

Of course the other prerequisite is a love of all things automotive and an enthusiasm for the whole concept of the console game as a serious entertainment medium. Kazunori goes on, "The new faces are generally those (programmers and designers) who were with us before, working part-time. We get them started and accustomed to the GT style of development, and they begin by getting used to the development tools and environments by modeling the cars."

Polyphony Digital Inc. was established in April 1998, as a 100% subsidiary of Sony Computer Entertainment Inc. The company started with just 30 staff to produce their first hit, Gran Turismo. With each subsequent version of GT, the size of the core team remained roughly the same. It was only during the development of GT4—with its increased number of cars, tracks and new technology—that the core team began to fluctuate between 60 and 70. And fewer than 10 or so handle development support and business relations. The core team roughly breaks down as follows:

• 20 engineers—primarily programmers who deal with three different areas: car physics, the 3D graphics engine, and linking the entire game together. Ten top programmers handle the main coding. They have to be versatile and understand every aspect of the game's development.
• 20 landscape designers—their task is to research and gather data on the race tracks, including the thousands of photographs required, and then go on to recreate them in the game's environment.
• 20 car modelers—their tasks are similar to the landscape designers, except of course they study and build the vehicles.
• Five movie-sequence staff—they storyboard, virtually film, and edit all of the FMV (full motion video) sequences used in the game's introduction and for marketing purposes.

• Three graphic designers—responsible for designing the many introduction, navigation, and selection screens to ensure GT has a cohesive style. They also handle the overall look of associated print, such as covers and manuals and marketing material.

Working at Polyphony takes a special kind of discipline, which although common across the games industry, is at variance with other creative media. Essentially it is the dynamic of a sizable team working on a single project for years. All areas of the project are deeply interlinked, particularly in programming, and rely very much on the team functioning well together at a consistent pace. Staff at Polyphony eat, breathe, and sleep GT.

WORKING ON A LONG-TERM GAMES PROJECT SUCH AS GRAN
TURISMO REQUIRES DEDICATED AND WELL-ORGANIZED
TEAMS, WHO ARE NOT ONLY EXPERTS IN THEIR SPECIFIC
FIELDS, BUT WHO CAN ALSO LINK WELL WITH THE GAME'S
OTHER AREAS OF DEVELOPMENT.

1. There were periods during GT4's three-year development when staff had to put in many working hours—meeting deadlines, preparing for Expos, or just keeping every department up to speed. Sometimes it just isn't worth going home.

2. Everywhere there are development versions of the game set up for testing.

3. Alongside the leisure equipment is a well-stocked library of books and video games.

4. The engine room.

5. Welcome to Polyphony. From the moment you cross the threshold, there are cars everywhere.

02 GRID

THE DREAM
THE DESIGN CHALLENGE FOR GT4

036

GT4 WAS ALWAYS GOING TO BE A TOUGH DESIGN CHALLENGE. HOW COULD POLYPHONY IMPROVE ON GT3—A GAME THAT HAD ALREADY ACHIEVED TECHNICAL BRILLIANCE? OTHER QUESTIONS WERE RAISED: HOW COULD GAME PLAY BE EXTENDED? HOW WOULD A NEW GT SUPPORT AND SATISFY A VIRTUAL-DRIVING AUDIENCE WHOSE NEW SKILLS HAD BEEN HONED ON THE PREVIOUS GT TITLES?

THE GAMES INDUSTRY WAITED WITH GREAT ANTICIPATION TO SEE HOW POLYPHONY COULD POSSIBLY IMPROVE ON THE ALREADY BRILLIANT GT3.

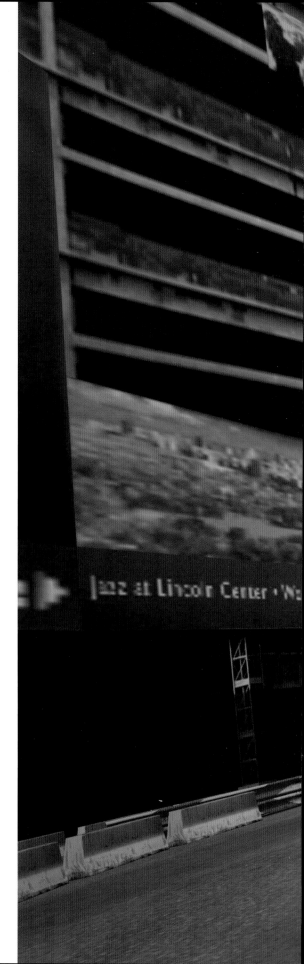

The Mercedes SL55 AMG takes a corner in front of the beautifully rendered Lincoln Center, New York.

1

3

2

4

1. The Toyota MTRC concept car. Including the latest advances in car design ensures the GT series always has fresh content.

2. New York City. Along with new tracks, some older ones would be revisited, but with a new level of fidelity.

3. The Toyota Sera drives through Paris, France. Automotive history would provide a rich pool of new content for GT, along with celebrating the technical and creative achievements of car designers.

4. The Toyota Celica GT-Four cornering on the Grand Canyon circuit. A whole new physics and graphics engine guaranteed to impress.

The challenge was great. Could Polyphony produce a sequel that would inject enough new elements to produce the same "wow" factor enjoyed by GT4's precursors, when gamers already knew what to expect from the series? And the PS2 itself, although a stunningly capable piece of hardware, has its limits. Could enough extra power be squeezed out of its silicon to make the title viable?

At the beginning of development the answer to these questions could only be guessed at—but with highly informed guesses, based on a foundation of knowledge gleaned from the experience of previous GT titles. Kazunori's ethos for the series, of a natural evolution towards technical perfection, provided the guiding light—but the road would not be so straightforward. The team couldn't take the existing code from GT3 and modify it here and there, perhaps bolting on the odd new feature, because it would simply become too cumbersome for the PS2. Ultimately it would fail the final lap when loyal fans, expecting more, would be disappointed with a few go-faster stripes on last year's model. Development had to return to the drawing board to create a new, faster, leaner game engine that would use every spare clock-cycle the PS2 had to offer in the most efficient way possible.

For the content, the cars, tracks and races, Kazunori had plenty to draw from in the form of his own dreams. There were so many cars and tracks he personally wanted to try and in many combinations of races. Also, with almost the entire real-world automotive industry keen to be involved, there would be no shortage of vehicles to populate the grid.

039

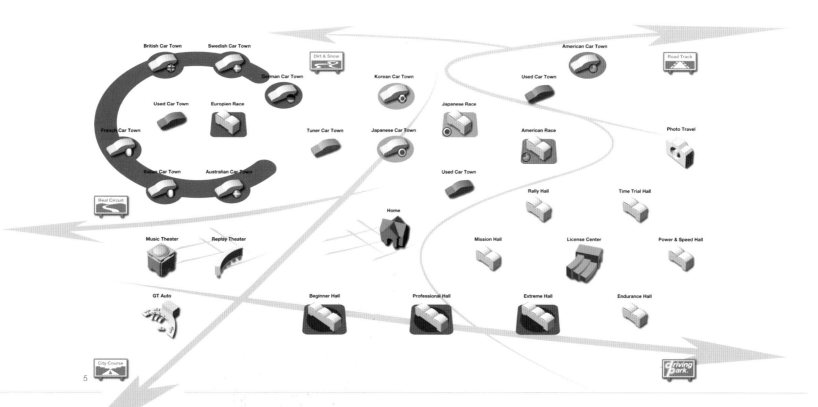

5. A diagram of the game's selection choices. With so many options available to the player, designing a coherent game interface can become extremely complex.

(Overleaf) The Mini Cooper S, shown off in the graphical splendor of Photo Mode.

PRODUCING A SEQUEL TO GT3 THAT WOULD PROVIDE GAMERS WITH THE SAME "WOW" FACTOR AS PREVIOUS VERSIONS WAS A HUGE TECHNICAL CHALLENGE. AN ENTIRELY NEW GAME ENGINE WAS NEEDED IF POLYPHONY WERE GOING TO GET CLOSE TO KAZUNORI'S DREAM.

041

FAST CARS #2

THE LE MANS 24 HOUR IS ONE OF THE MOST DEMANDING RACES IN THE WORLD. TO WIN, CARS HAVE TO BE DESIGNED TO THE HIGHEST SPECIFICATION.

042

VITAL STATISTICS: COURAGE 60

MAX POWER:	510 bhp @ 6500 rpm	**LENGTH:**	4.64 m	**ENGINE TYPE:**	V6/DOHC
MAX TORQUE:	657 Nm @ 5000 rpm	**TOTAL WIDTH:**	1.99 m	**ASPIRATION TYPE:**	Twin Turbo
DISPLACEMENT:	3200 cc	**WHEEL BASE:**	2.54 m	**POWER/WEIGHT RATIO:**	0.57 bhp/kg
WEIGHT:	900 kg	**TREAD (FRONT):**	N/A	**TORQUE/WEIGHT RATIO:**	0.73 Nm/kg
HEIGHT:	N/A	**TREAD (REAR):**	N/A	**ARCADE MODE:**	YES

In 1972 Henri Pescarolo and Graham Hill won Le Mans in a French car, the Matra-Simca MS670, dispelling the fear that a French team could never win. Pescarolo gained hero status with three more wins before retiring from active racing and returning to Le Mans as a team manager. His first car used a Courage C52 chassis with a modified Peugeot engine—all French, as were his drivers. Results in the 2000 Le Mans were disappointing: they lost out to the better-funded Audi team.

Pescarolo bought the Courage 60 chassis for the 2001 Le Mans, but owing to mechanical problems, a crash, and rain, the team only managed to reach 13th place. Approaching the Le Mans 2002, Pescarolo hired André de Cortanze to design the new C60. Cortanze made a number of modifications to the C60's sleek body shape and for 2003 a Bentley Speed-8 engine was introduced. The model pictured here, sponsored by Sony PlayStation, runs with the Judd engine in 2004.

03 GREEN
COLLECTING THE DATA

044

BEHIND THE AWESOME GRAPHICS AND ADRENALIN-INDUCING PHYSICS ARE BILLIONS OF 0s AND 1s, AND EACH ONE HAS TO BE RIGHT. OF COURSE POLYPHONY WORKED AT A HIGHER LEVEL THAN BINARY WHILE COLLECTING THE MASS OF DATA REQUIRED FOR A GAME SUCH AS GT4. BUT TALKING IN TERMS OF THE SMALLEST DIGITAL COMPONENT TRULY REFLECTS THE LEVEL OF DETAIL FOR WHICH THEY WERE STRIVING.

THE VAST AMOUNT OF DATA COLLECTED, FROM VEHICLE PERFORMANCE FIGURES TO THOUSANDS OF TRACK SURFACE PHOTOGRAPHS, ALL HAD TO BE FILTERED AND CHECKED INTO ORGANIZED DATABASES.

The Toyota Sera gull wing 1992 concept virtually photographed in the Kokusai Forum, Tokyo.

1. Preparation for a test drive.

CAR DATA
RECORDING THE VITAL STATISTICS

047

GATHERING DATA FOR GT4 MUST BE EVERY AUTO-ENTHUSIAST'S DREAM JOB—THE CHANCE TO STUDY SOME OF THE MOST EXCITING PERFORMANCE CARS IN DETAIL. MODERN VEHICLE MANUFACTURERS HELPED BY PROVIDING CAD AND TELEMETRIC DATA. THE ONLY MAJOR PROBLEM CAME WHEN TRACKING DOWN ACCURATE DATA ON HISTORICAL MODELS.

2

3

2. Kazunori with members of the team discussing the day's data collection tasks.
3. A Mitsubishi Lancer Evolution VII being used in the creation of Gran Turismo.

OFTEN THE DATA-GATHERING TEAMS HAD TO TRAVEL ALL OVER THE GLOBE IN SEARCH OF SPECIFIC CAR MODELS. THE RESULT IS A UNIQUE COLLECTION OF VEHICLES; STEPPING STONES THROUGH AUTOMOTIVE HISTORY.

048

Data collection breaks down into two distinct areas: physics data (the car's performance and handling) and visual data (the car's appearance). In both areas a lot of material can be gathered from manufacturer's specifications, drawings, and photographs. However, Polyphony are keen to check every detail and experience the vehicle in real life, thereby capturing the 'feel' of the car.

Kazunori describes how a car's visual form is recorded and recreated in the game: 'We conduct a photo shooting session for the car by taking lots of photos. Roughly 500 photos are taken per car. For a normal street car (those available to us on the market), the team will take photos of the whole car, each of its details, long distance shots, all of the lights, and the interior. With race cars, we then add the process of gathering details on the livery (stickers and so forth). Then, based on these photos the car-modeling designers start modeling each car as if they are working on a piece of sculpture. It is almost like taking a large piece of marble, and creating the statue of David, by Michelangelo.'

While test driving can be useful during data collection, it's not essential. Kazunori says, 'Ideally, I would love to test drive all of the cars included in GT. I would like to mention, however, that it is not a "must-do" process in order to create the cars for the game. With GT, we adhere to creating a given car's performance by collecting and utilizing objective parameters of the car (for instance the total weight, weight on the front/rear axle and so on). We would not have been able to create GT if we had to rely on a test-driving procedure for each car to begin with.'

Test driving covers not only the vehicle's basic performance data but several other factors. 'Examples of data gathered when test driving a car would be the varying speed of the car in given conditions, force of gravity in all 4 directions (front, rear, left, right), sound, and so on', adds Kazunori.

The way a car behaves is subject to hundreds of variables that break down into three main areas; the car's on-paper specification, the external conditions (such as track surface and weather), and—of course—the driver.

1

3

2

4

TO MAKE THE CARS APPEAR AS REAL AS THEY DO IN-GAME IS NO LUCKY ACCIDENT. THOUSANDS OF PHOTOGRAPHS AND TERRABYTES OF DATA ARE COLLECTED AND COLLATED TO ENSURE THAT WHAT THE PLAYERS SEE DURING THE GAME IS AS CLOSE AS POSSIBLE TO THE REAL THING.

1. The team inspect a Lotus Esprit during a road test of several cars.

2. Data-recording equipment is varied and sophisticated.

3. Everything is recorded down to the finest details.

4. The Polyphony team brought together their own cars for road testing at the Motegi Track.

5

6

5. Photographing details. The triangle on the right is used to compare relative positions on this Audi and ensure correct scaling when measurements are taken from the photographs.

6. More turn up. The opportunity to drive some of the world's super-cars is one of the perks of the job.

03 GREEN

TRACK DATA

MEASURING THE GREATEST CIRCUITS IN THE WORLD

050

HALF OF THE 50 TRACKS IN GT ARE BASED ON REAL LOCATIONS. TO SAY 'BASED', HOWEVER, UNDERVALUES THE FACT THAT THEY ARE METER-FOR-METER ACCURATE DIGITAL RECREATIONS. FOR POLYPHONY THE ENVIRONMENT IN WHICH YOU RACE IS AS IMPORTANT AS THE CARS—THE EXPERIENCE OF ONE IS WHOLLY DEPENDENT ON THE OTHER.

1

'ONE EXAMPLE OF A TRIP FOR STAGE ONE OF DEVELOPMENT WOULD BE A GROUP OF FIVE TO SEVEN PEOPLE TRAVELING TO AREAS OF EUROPE, NORTH AMERICA, OR ASIA FOR A PERIOD OF UP TO TWO MONTHS. GENERALLY SPEAKING, THREE TEAMS TRAVEL AROUND THE WORLD TO COLLECT MATERIALS.'
KAZUNORI YAMAUCHI

1. Collecting data at the Grand Canyon. While spectacular, photographing every square meter of such a huge landform, is taxing and complex work.

2. Cranes were used to elevate the camera to allow perpendicular shots of the track surface to be used directly as in-game textures.

PLOTTING THE TRACKS AND CIRCUITS THAT APPEAR IN GT4
IN SUCH RESPLENDENT REALISM IS A PAINSTAKING TASK
THAT RELIES ON THOUSANDS OF STILL PHOTOGRAPHS AND
VIDEO FOOTAGE.

1. The tracks were all filmed and the footage compared to the in-game digital version.

2. Citta di Aria in Assisi, Italy. Every environment has to be methodically surveyed and photographed.

3. Distant horizons have to be photographed 360° for mapping onto the track's background. Citta di Aria required the collection of a massive 50,000 photographs during a two-week period on location.

053

The basis of the track research starts with photographs, 20–30,000 of them for each individual circuit. The photographs perform several different functions. Some are linked into surveying the circuit's topography, recording the three-dimensional shape of the land through which the track twists and turns. Often a member of the team is photographed holding long measuring sticks against crash barriers or unidentifiable trackside buildings. These photographs allow such roadside elements to be checked for accuracy once they've been designed into the game back at Polyphony's studios. Even apparently small details are collected, such as the few centimetres between pit entry lines painted on the tarmac.

The majority of photographs are used directly in the game as surface textures to be mapped onto the polygons that make GT's virtual world. The scale of this task is humbling.

Essentially, every square metre of the track has to be photographed and the image logged and linked to its exact position on the track. Trackside buildings receive the same attention, each face photographed from as perpendicular an angle as possible to prevent distortion. The number of buildings that require photographing in this way can be surprisingly large, particularly in cities, as different views from the circuit can open up long perspectives down streets, even though the track passes them by. Such photographs also have to be taken in overcast lighting conditions without strong shadows which would look unnaturally fixed if they appeared in-game.

The team also makes use of satellite photographs combined with GPS (Global Positioning Satellite) and existing topographical maps. Finally, the middle and far distance must then be photographed in segments around the entire visible compass.

4. All buildings if visible from the track, as most are, have to be correctly plotted and recorded.

5. The Grand Canyon is the deepest three-dimensional location reproduced in the game.

054

1

To stop and concentrate on any track scene, even on visually uncluttered circuits such as Fuji, reveals a huge list of details. These range from a barely noticed electrical-services box to serried ranks of advertising hoardings. Even things as mundane as wire-mesh fencing and crowd barriers are particular to any specific location. There are crash barriers, track lamps, oil barrels, piles of tires, trash cans, electricity pylons, access gates—the list is endless. All of these items are measured, photographed and then stored. It is critical to get these details right to complete the authenticity and to avoid the tiled, repetitive backgrounds sometimes seen in other games.

Team members must also attend race events at the circuits to take photographs of the location when it is being used for race days. On these occasions there are new details to capture, from hot-dog stands to temporary champion's podia, and of course, the crowds, whose manner, ethnic mix, and dress all vary depending on where in the world the event is held. There are elements of the race itself that have to be noted, such as how the cars line up on the starting grid or how many pit crew members are milling around waiting to change tires.

Finally, there is the intangible data that is difficult to quantify. It lies in the different quality of light, for example the way dust hangs behind a car in the Grand Canyon is different to the splatters of mud from a rain-sodden rally track. Of course recording the effects of weather on the track are also critical. For some tracks, such as those set in the snow, the weather is central to the whole driving experience while other effects, such as heat haze on the climb into a Mediterranean village, just complete the atmosphere.

ANOTHER VARIABLE THAT WAS TAKEN INTO ACCOUNT WAS THAT CARS SOUND DIFFERENT DEPENDING ON THE TRACK. THE 'TRACK SIGNATURE' HAD TO BE CAREFULLY RECORDED AND ANALYZED SO THAT IT'S REPLICATED ACCURATELY IN-GAME.

1. For everything to do with GT, the most up-to-date equipment was used.

2

4

3

5

2. With photographs being required from every angle the teams needed access to every part of the tracks and surrounding land.

3. Data collecting at Nürburgring. Mapping progress.

4. Even the most mundane trackside paraphernalia is measured, photographed and stored.

5. Keeping on top of the logistics of collection and the mass of data generated requires good organization.

03 GREEN

WORKING WITH MANUFACTURERS

USING GENUINE DESIGN DATA

056

Kazunori describes how Polyphony's relationship with car makers has changed during the creation of the various versions of GT: 'In the past, the selection of cars was a selection of those I wanted in the game. 100%. As the franchise moved forward, car manufacturers have begun to request or suggest certain models to be included in the game. From my point of view, I wish to pay my gratitude to the car manufacturers who have continued to create the great masterpieces called cars in one way or another. I also hope that their cars do well in the market (sell), and for the same reasons, I would like to try and fulfill their requests as much as possible.'

Gran Turismo began with just 10 car manufacturers providing their support. Some of these were small, such as TVR, with only a handful of major manufacturers wanting to associate themselves with a video game. Now manufacturers are more keen than ever to be associated with the prestigious GT. What better way to promote their products to the 'PlayStation generation', a large section of their market who are now out of reach of traditional TV advertising?

Some manufacturers, such as BMW, are so used to working with Polyphony that they can tailor their car's data-collection systems for direct insertion into the GT game engine. Equally, Polyphony have provided specially modified versions of the game for manufacturers who want to test their concepts to the limits in a safe virtual environment. Surely the ultimate vindication, if any were needed, of the precision of the GT physics engine.

1

2

3

IT IS INTERESTING TO NOTE THAT GT HAS ALWAYS BEEN
PEPPERED WITH CONCEPT CARS THAT ARE FUN AND
ATTRACTIVE TO PLAYERS. THEIR INCLUSION ALSO ALLOWS
THE CAR MAKERS TO TEST THE LEVEL OF ACCEPTANCE AND
PLAN FUTURE DESIGN DIRECTION.

4

Isolated renders of GT cars. With this quality of realism manufacturers can use GT not only to test performance but also consider the appearance of the styling in different locations.

1. BMW 1 Series, 2004.

2. RUF RGT, 2000.

3. TVR Tuscan Speed 6, 2000.

4. A BMW McLaren F1 GTR, 1997.

BMW continue a tradition of building quality cars with an emphasis on style, performance and technological advance.

BMW
A CLASSIC DESIGN PEDIGREE

The world-famous car manufacturer, BMW, was one of the first to supply licensed cars for use in Gran Turismo, and the company has enjoyed a mutually beneficial relationship with Polyphony. Like most car makers they initially considered video games as novelty toys—a million miles away from real car technologies. However, the success of Gran Turismo with its huge sales persuaded BMW of its undoubted ability to put their cars in front of a new generation of buyers.

It wasn't long before Polyphony and BMW began to work closely together, sharing knowledge of car development and technology. As work on the new GT4 physics engine proceeded BMW were interested in Polyphony developing a version specifically to test the performance of their new car designs. While standard real-life tests still take place BMW found they were able to use the GT4 game engine to test their cars' performance to the limits without endangering the lives of their real-life test drivers.

BMW sees the relationship continuing in a number of ways as the GT game engine continues to mature. Apart from testing the new cars' performance, BMW can set up virtual trials for prospective customers to take test drives. In addition, concept cars' styling and market position can be interactively presented to marketing focus groups for feedback. This synergy between the companies shows how the once frivolous image of video games is changing in the eyes of big established 'gold' industries.

059

BMW are represented in GT4 with 13 different models including the 1 and 3 series, the exciting M3 GTR race car and a taste of the future with the M5 concept.

BMW (BAYERISCHE MOTORENWERKE) WAS THE RESULT OF THE MERGING OF TWO AIRPLANE ENGINE MAKERS IN 1916. APART FROM CARS BUILT UNDER LICENSE THEIR FIRST 'REAL' BMW CAR WAS THE AM4, PRODUCED IN 1932.

FAST CARS #3

THE ELISE, WITH INNOVATIVE
TECHNOLOGY AND LOTUS DESIGN,
WAS A PERFECT COMBINATION OF
EXCELLENT PERFORMANCE AND
WONDERFULLY GOOD LOOKS.

LOTUS ELISE

060

VITAL STATISTICS: LOTUS ELISE

MAX POWER:	118 bhp @ 5500 rpm	*LENGTH:*	3.726 m	*ENGINE TYPE:*	1.8 litre/Straight 4
MAX TORQUE:	165 Nm @ 3000 rpm	*TOTAL WIDTH:*	1.7 m	*ASPIRATION TYPE:*	Normal
DISPLACEMENT:	1796 cc	*WHEEL BASE:*	2.3 m	*POWER/WEIGHT RATIO:*	0.17 bhp/kg
WEIGHT:	690 kg	*TREAD (FRONT):*	1.44 m	*TORQUE/WEIGHT RATIO:*	0.24 Nm/kg
HEIGHT:	1.2 m	*TREAD (REAR):*	1.453 m	*ARCADE MODE:*	YES

The Elise was the first car to be released by Lotus after the Italian entrepreneur Roman Artioli had bought the company from General Motors. The designers based the car on an innovative bonded-aluminium spaceframe, which, along with the composite material body, resulted in an extraordinarily light car. Initially the car shipped with a 118-bhp engine, which many thought would prove underpowered. However, the power to weight ratio was excellent and the car performed and handled extremely well.

When it was released at the Frankfurt motorshow toward the end of 1995 it found acclaim with both the public and the press. Over 14,000 were produced including a number of special editions such as the 111, the Sport 160, pictured above, and the track-only race car, the Sport 190 (see left). Production of the original ceased in 2000 and the Elise flame was handed over to a revised Series 2.

04 TORQUE
VEHICLE PHYSICS

062

UNDER THE HOOD OF GT LIES THE PHYSICS ENGINE. ALL OF THE PHYSICAL ELEMENTS YOU WOULD EXPECT TO AFFECT A VEHICLE IN MOTION HAVE BEEN STUDIED AND MAPPED. WORKING CONSTANTLY IN THE BACKGROUND, THE ENGINE PERFORMS MILLIONS OF CALCULATIONS, ADJUSTING THE CAR'S POSITION IN RESPONSE TO THE DRIVER'S ACTIONS AND THE FORCES ACTING UPON IT.

"I WOULDN'T SAY THE PHYSICS ENGINE IS COMPLETE, BUT SO FAR WE HAVE SPENT 12 YEARS ON IT."
KAZUNORI YAMAUCHI

The 1967 Shelby Cobra 427 had it all—astonishing performance, aggressive good looks, and a thunderous engine note.

3

1

2

1-2. The real 2204 PlayStation Pescarolo C60 LMP Judd. Race cars have the same physics applied to them as production cars, it's just the parameters that are extreme.

3. The Peugeot 205 Turbo 16 Evolution 2 Group B rally car. Assessing a rally car's physics is more difficult because of the unpredictability of external forces in the driving environment.

REAL-CAR PHYSICS

The detail of automotive physics forms a huge subject in itself, but can be understood in a simplified form by focusing on longitudinal forces—direct forward and reverse motion—and latitude, the forces that allow the car to turn.

The main longitudinal force is the forward force of the engine, against which is an array of negative forces such as rolling and mechanical resistance and, most important of all, aerodynamic drag or wind resistance. Add these factors up at any given time and the result is the car's speed. The engine's forward momentum is initially a rotational force, a torque, to the car's drive wheels which causes them to push backward on the road surface. This is called traction.

Unimpeded the car would accelerate infinitely, but as it gathers speed so the opposite force of aerodynamic drag increases. The other main resistance, particularly at slow speeds, is rolling resistance, caused by friction between the rubber and the road surface, and friction in the mechanics of the car itself. So long as an engine can deliver enough power to overcome these forces it will accelerate to the point where it fails—this is the car's maximum velocity.

When turning, different lateral forces are in play at low speed and at high speed. At low speed there is little forward velocity so the car will follow the rolling direction of the wheels. Forcing the car to turn at higher speeds is achieved by the tires' increased friction with the road surface, which increasingly comes into direct competition with the car's forward impetus. Skidding occurs when the tires' friction effects fail.

4

5

4. Toyota GT1 TS020. Collecting data from race cars requires working closely with the race team as the cars are non-standard and heavily modified.

5. Nissan 350Z. The Nürburgring track was designed to test automobile physics to the limit.

REAL-CAR PHYSICS ARE FANTASTICALLY COMPLICATED, BUT HAVE BEEN ORGANIZED INTO MATHEMATICAL FORMULAE USED BY CAR MANUFACTURERS AND GAMES PROGRAMMERS ALIKE.

04 TORQUE

PHYSICS DATA COLLECTION

066

EACH CAR IN GRAN TURISMO 4 IS SUBJECT TO OVER 300 DIFFERENT PHYSICS CALCULATIONS. EACH CALCULATION HAS TO HAVE THE CORRECT DATA TO WORK WITH, AND EACH OF THESE HAS PARAMETERS, SUCH AS A MINIMUM, MAXIMUM, AND RATE OF TRAVEL. ALL OF THESE PARAMETERS HAVE TO BE RESEARCHED AND RECORDED.

GT4 FEATURES MANY OLDER VEHICLES, INCLUDING THE FIRST MASS-PRODUCED CAR, THE FORD MODEL T, FROM 1914, FOR WHICH DETAILED PHYSICS DATA IS NO LONGER AVAILABLE.

1-2. Sometimes the team had to work through many cars in a single session because of the limited time available on test tracks.

The starting point for physics data collection was the manufacturers' own data. This worked well for cars built in the last couple of decades as the makers were used to keeping and storing documents. Some car specifications were harder to track down because the company had gone out of business, such as De Lorean, or been subsumed into larger conglomerates where data on even relatively recent vehicles had got lost along the way.

Not all manufacturers had tested their cars for all of the physical data under different conditions that Polyphony needed. This was particularly true of older models, and while the main performance data was well-known, Polyphony had to rig their own tests to gather the detail they required. Some of these cars were so old they had to be coaxed from their retirement museums out onto the test track.

Race cars introduced new challenges for the data-collection teams. Some had a very limited production run while others were unique, individual cars heavily modified by the race team. Because their specifications changed from one race to the next, the team had to pin down the specific build they wanted to concentrate on, freezing the car's ongoing evolution. When it came to testing, the team requested the aid of professional race drivers, the only drivers able to truly harness their power.

In its selection of vehicles GT4 comes right up to the present and beyond, covering the latest releases and looking into the future with concept cars. Many of these vehicles were not finalized themselves during the three years the game took to complete, so their in-game versions often needed adjustment to ensure they were up-to-date. Kazunori explains, "Each time a car manufacturer announces a new mechanism and a thesis is submitted we then study and add the new mechanism to our simulation model."

1

2

3. Although his face is obscured, this is Kazunori setting off on a test drive. He is an excellent driver in his own right.

4. A film crew runs through footage in the field.

5. Kazunori and his team examine each car, both for details and its "feel."

IN-GAME PHYSICS HANDLING

COMPUTING THE DATA

069

THE PHYSICS ENGINE IS A MACHINE. FROM GT1 IT HAS BEEN IN CONSTANT EVOLUTION, BEING REDESIGNED, REBUILT, REFINED, AND FINELY TUNED. IT HAS TO PERFORM RELIABLY AND AT SPEED. DATA IS PUMPED INTO IT, ADJUSTED, CHECKED, READJUSTED, AND TRANSLATED INTO MINUTE MOVEMENTS OF THE CAR, ALL IN A MATTER OF HUNDREDTHS OF A SECOND.

A Honda NSX GT500 in among the competition at the Fuji race circuit.

THE PHYSICS ENGINE IS THE PART OF THE GAME'S PROGRAM THAT SIMULATES THE EFFECTS OF REAL-WORLD PHYSICS IN THE GAME ENVIRONMENT.

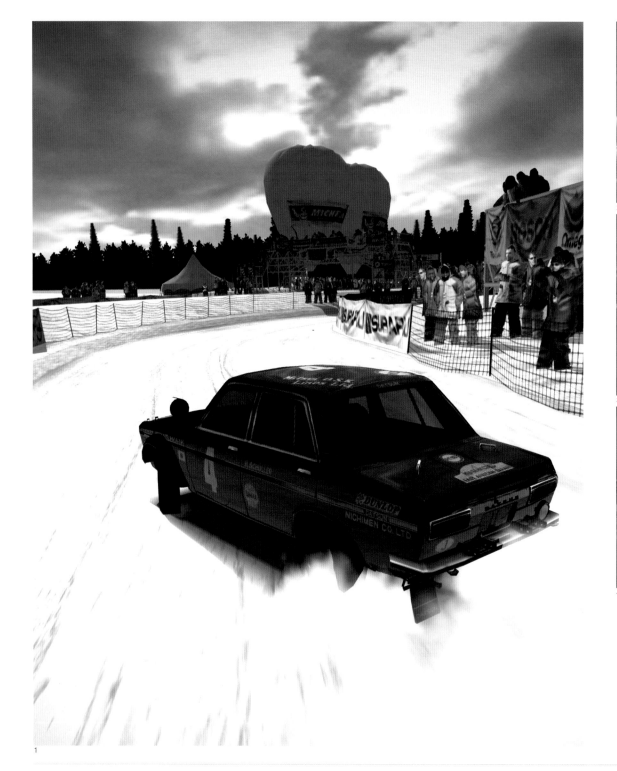

1. A 1969 Nissan Bluebird 1600 SSS on GT4's ice rally. The physics engine copes with a wide variety of road and weather conditions.

2. The PlayStation Pescarolo C60 LMR Judd. The physics engine accurately handles performance data from race cars that themselves are pushing the boundaries of automotive science.

3. A Lancia Stratos powering up a steep section of the Citta di Aria circuit.

4. Dodge Viper SRT/5. The level of realism means that advanced driving techniques such as the power-slide are possible.

5. A Type 1 Volkswagen 1100 Standard Beetle (1949) in Photo Mode. Even at rest, physics have to be accounted for—note the weight of the car realistically compressing the tires.

6. The physics engine, though tooled to drive the latest high-performance cars, works just as well in the Model-T Ford. Note how clearly the driver is visible.

The simulation of real-world physical effects is at the center of most current game development, with the creation of a single working model that can support virtual actors as its goal. Polyphony have been working with a similar concept in mind for GT, except focusing on cars. Kazunori sees the engine as a grand project that is constantly in development.

GT4's engine has to be flexible enough to cope with all the extremes of data from different cars. It does this using a "soft", object-oriented approach, where any car's data can be applied and it will recreate that car's performance and handling digitally. While broad in its capacity it must also be as efficient as possible at processing the data, for processor cycles are very valuable and any bottleneck here would affect the entire performance of the game.

Kazunori describes the extent of the game physics engine: "In total there are hundreds of parameters we use. Some examples would be the weight of the car, the torque curve of the engine's performance, and many others."

The engine has been honed over the whole life of the series. Kazunori concedes that while highly sophisticated, the engine cannot currently replicate absolutely every force at play in the real world: "Since our physics is still immature there are times we must reduce the realism."

In practise the discrepancies with the real world are so small that they are imperceptible during play.

And even taking into account these tiny discrepancies, the level of detail is astonishing: "In regards to simulating the damping on a car's suspension, yes we do calculate and simulate the overall damping rate, but this does not yet go to the extent of simulating each individual damper and its individual stroke speed. As for the four-wheel-drive systems, yes we do simulate each and every system differently."

7

071

5

6

8

7. A 1995 Celica GT-Four rally car. While striving for realism, the engine is also adjustable to provide more accessible, fun driving in arcade mode. Driving aids such as traction control can be turned on, even in older cars that didn't have this option.

8. A Ford GT with Gran Turismo branding leads on the Yosemite track.

"WE DON'T NECESSARILY HAVE A TOP PROGRAMMER. WE DO HAVE ABOUT 10 'CREAM OF THE CROP' PROGRAMMERS WHO DYNAMICALLY TACKLE THEIR TASKS, AND WHO ALL JUMP INTO THESE TASKS TO BRING THE PRODUCT TOWARD COMPLETION."
KAZUNORI YAMAUCHI

04 TORQUE
THE BALANCE
REAL LIFE AND GAME PLAY

072

1

2

FINDING THE PERFECT POINT OF BALANCE IN A COMPUTER GAME IS ALWAYS DIFFICULT. KAZUNORI HAS TO SATISFY EXPERIENCED GT PLAYERS, WHO ARE LOOKING FOR A CHALLENGE, WHILE STILL ACCOMMODATING BOTH THE NOVICE AND THE CASUAL GAMER.

Interestingly Kazunori doesn't see any necessity to tone down reality for the novice. Instead he uses reality, in the form of driving lessons, to teach novices how to drive: "For the beginners, there are license tests set up within game play, where they can learn about driving, and by providing features such as driver-assisting technology this can help players reduce the dangers of missing the track. The driver-assist technology is further enhanced in GT4, allowing players to drive fast, yet safe even when the driver-assist is in action. This is in sync with the advancements in technology for safety devices available on real road cars. ABS, TCS, EBD, ESP and others are scheduled to be combined and implemented."

The casual driver has been catered for from the beginning of the series with arcade mode. Here the physics engine is intentionally turned down to make handling even the wildest of cars easier.

WIDE AUDIENCE APPEAL IS IMPORTANT COMMERCIALLY BUT FOR KAZUNORI IT ALSO REFLECTS HIS DESIRE NOT TO BAR ANYONE WHO WANTS TO GET BEHIND THE STEERING WHEEL AND ENJOY THE WONDERS OF GT.

1. The great success of Gran Turismo as a series is that it appeals to a wide audience by catering to the experienced and welcoming the novice.

2. With realism at its heart GT has also attracted driving enthusiasts who would otherwise never have approached a video game.

3. A Dodge Viper SRT 10, 2003 and Mercedes SL55 AMG battle it out on the streets of New York. Balance is also about selecting the right opponents, as players want some hope of a victory. Thus matching classes of driver is important both with AI drivers and multiplayer leagues.

1

KAZUNORI, WITH HIS INSISTENCE ON REALISM, DOES NOT
WANT TO COMPROMISE WITH IMPRESSIONS OF THE EFFECTS
OF A CRASH. INSTEAD POLYPHONY CONTINUE TO RESEARCH
AND DEVELOP THE REAL PHYSICS OF IMPACT DAMAGE.

1. Force feedback steering wheels with a gear lever and
pedals are the best way to experience GT.

For the more experienced drivers, Kazunori knows that the pursuit of realism will always provide enough of a challenge. After all, real-world racing is no less challenging to real-world drivers. Kazunori explains, "For the core or seasoned veterans, I am sure they will follow the simple philosophy of GT—the importance of high-quality reality."

There are limits, though, where reality interferes with game play. Some aspects of driving, particularly high-speed racing, where the cars sometimes exceed their mechanical limits, can interrupt the joy of racing itself. Kazunori sees it as a very difficult balance to strike: "Real cars are great fun to drive. For the same reasons, I have faith that if we continue to pursue the simulation of reality, the game play will definitely be something fun or enjoyable. Looking specifically at the driving aspect, the higher the reality gets, the higher the fun or excitement will be. I think this assumption is correct. However,

bringing reality levels high for all aspects, things are likely to become stressful, which is troublesome. For example, the brakes on a standard (stock) sports car, driven at a race track for three laps, will start to lose their performance. Perhaps the brakes will last another three laps if the car is equipped with more powerful brake kits. With some cars, taking it around the track at full speed for ten laps may ruin the engine. If a car driving at 250 km/h just slightly hits a sidewall, there is actually a force of 200 Gs and the car would disintegrate into millions of pieces of metal. The question and problem is, do we replicate reality to these extents where reality is 'unfavorable' for the players?"

Regardless of these concerns, Polyphony continues to research and develop all areas of vehicle physics in the pursuit of absolute realism. Even if some aspects can be turned off by the player, Kazunori knows that GT should always have the capacity to offer the same challenges found in real-world racing.

075

2

4

6

3

5

7

2. The Mazda Demio. While the physics engine is based on reality the game must still deliver a fun experience.

3. A Saleen S7 in Las Vegas. Fast cars are difficult to handle in GT and beginners have a tendency to spin them out while driving on straights. Real-life steering correction technologies can be switched on to avoid this.

4. A Toyota V300 enjoying the Paris street circuit.

5. A Nissan Exa Canopy L.A. Version Type S flashes past spectators during a Paris street circuit race.

6. Another view of the Paris circuit, this time featuring a Mazda Cosmo Sport (L10A) dating from 1967.

7. A BMW M5 tearing through the Citta di Aria track.

FAST CARS #4

TOYOTA MTRC

TOYOTA'S ANSWER TO A NEW GENERATION USED TO HIGH-TECH GADGETS, THE MTRC IS DESIGNED TO SUIT OFF-ROAD RACING AND CITY STREETS ALL IN ONE PACKAGE.

076

VITAL STATISTICS: TOYOTA MTRC

MAX POWER:	N/A	LENGTH:	N/A	ENGINE TYPE:	N/A
MAX TORQUE:	N/A	TOTAL WIDTH:	N/A	ASPIRATION TYPE:	N/A
DISPLACEMENT:	N/A	WHEEL BASE:	N/A	POWER/WEIGHT RATIO:	N/A
WEIGHT:	N/A	TREAD (FRONT):	N/A	TORQUE/WEIGHT RATIO:	N/A
HEIGHT:	N/A	TREAD (REAR):	N/A	ARCADE MODE:	YES

Concept cars have been an important part of a car manufacturer's research program. Although the designs look too exotic for current tastes, they point the way to new technologies and probe new stylistic avenues.

The MTRC was designed and built at Toyota's European design studio, ED2, with the "triathlon" idea of working in multiple environments. Where the car really points to the future is in its use of fuel cells to power the electric motors in each wheel, automatically providing four-wheel drive. Fuel-cell technology is currently a major area of research for all car manufacturers concerned with environmental damage from fossil fuels.

Of particular interest is the way that Toyota was able to include the car in GT4, giving the opportunity for millions to road test a car they would be very unlikely to experience otherwise.

05 BHP
3D GRAPHICS ENGINE

078

GRAN TURISMO IS VISUALLY STUNNING. NOT ONLY DOES IT RIVAL PHOTO REALISM, IT OFTEN SURPASSES IT. A BEAUTIFUL SUNSET IS MORE THAN A TEXTURE PAINTED ON A POLYGON BACKDROP, IT IS IN EVERYTHING AROUND YOU. SUN GLINTS FROM AN OPPONENT'S REAR WINDOW, DUST FROM THEIR TIRES BLURS THE RAYS, AND THE LIGHT SHIFTS IN THE LEAVES OF THE TREES.

ALTHOUGH THE GRAPHICS ENGINE WAS REWRITTEN FOR GT4, IT WAS THE EVOLUTION OF THE HUMAN DESIGNERS' SKILLS THAT WAS MAINLY RESPONSIBLE FOR THE HUGE IMPROVEMENT IN GRAPHICAL QUALITY.

The Renault Alpine A110 1600S virtually photographed against the Brooklyn Bridge in New York.

05 BHP
REAL-TIME 3D
HOW IT WORKS

1

2

080

PLAYING IN A COMPUTER-GENERATED 3D ENVIRONMENT IS COMMONPLACE IN MODERN GAMES AND IS INTEGRAL TO THE PLAYSTATION'S VISUAL-DISPLAY SYSTEM.

The process by which the PlayStation creates its image is similar to the way CGI (computer-generated imagery) is created in films such as Pixar's *Toy Story* and Square's *Final Fantasy—The Spirits Within*. It all starts with the creation of virtual three-dimensional models of the cars and tracks. These are built, by hand, in the computer from individual points that are then linked and filled to form polygons, finally creating an infinitely thin skin around the object. This is then "textured" with an image of the surface of the object. In the case of a car it would be made up of photographs from each side of the real car. Only the immediate area featured in the game needs to be built, and in a similar way to studio stage sets in movies, the background is mapped onto a dome covering the whole scene.

Lights and cameras are then placed in the scene. It is at this point that movie CGI and games diverge a little. Both "film" the scene through the virtual cameras, but games have to render each frame from the scene fast enough to display it instantly, because to make the game interactive it must respond to the user's actions in real-time. The speed of this loop—user action > changes position of scene objects > take image and pass it to the display (TV)—is critical to the final graphic quality of the game. The faster it works, the more detail, distance, special effects, shadows, and other visual phenomena from the natural world can be displayed.

3

TEXTURED POLYGONS ARE THE BASIC INGREDIENT OF GT4'S STUNNING VISUALS. OUT OF THEM THE WHOLE GAME ENVIRONMENT IS CREATED.

1. The Toyota Celica SS-II on the Las Vegas Drag strip. Some visual effects, such as the brake lights switching on, are created by swapping the surface texture image.

2. The Honda NSX Type S Zero at Las Vegas. Subtle lighting is critical for realism, particularly to avoid a "stagey" appearance.

3. The 1977 Lancia Stratos Group 4 rally car at the Ice Rally. Some effects, such as the semi-transparent snow effect, are aided by a function of the hardware display system.

4. The Nissan 89C at the Paris Rally. Effects such as the starburst from the car's headlights mimic the way camera lenses behave, adding to the photographic realism of the scene.

THE GT GRAPHICS ENGINE
THE 4TH DIMENSION

83

EVER SINCE THE LAUNCH OF THE FIRST GT, THE QUALITY OF THE GRAPHICS HAS AMAZED PLAYERS. GT4 SAW THE THIRD MAJOR REWRITE OF THE CORE GRAPHICS CODE. KAZUNORI EXPLAINS, "WE HAD NOT EXTRACTED ALL THERE WAS FROM THE PS2. WE HAVE RE-THOUGHT THE PROCEDURES AND RE-BUILT OUR TECHNOLOGY TO CREATE AN EVEN BETTER LOOKING GAME."

1. Two Peugeot 206s battling it out on the streets of Paris. The flare from the various lights adds to the illusion that players are watching a real televised race.
2. The Toyota TS020 screams through Paris.
3. A Chrysler SRT4 on the Las Vegas Drag Strip.

Look at all of the images on this page. Together they show the careful attention to the different atmospheres of each circuit, which is just as much a product of the artist's work as of the graphics engine.

GT4 PRODUCES AN ALMOST PHOTOGRAPHIC IMAGE. ALTHOUGH MOSTLY DOWN TO THE EFFORTS OF THE GT TEAM, IT IS HELPED BY THE PS2'S EXCEPTIONAL PIXEL-FILL RATE.

084

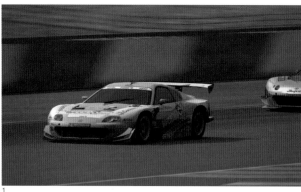

1

3

2

4

In one respect the staff at Polyphony were in an excellent position when they approached re-writing the graphics engine. They could build on extensive knowledge of the PS2 hardware from their work on GT3. At the same time they had to apply themselves to writing an extremely efficient engine to exploit the hardware to its limits. The details of their graphic techniques, perhaps more than any other area of the game, is a carefully guarded secret.

A close look at GT4 from a graphics engine programming point of view reveals the astonishing achievements of the team. The most obvious is distance. Each object, tree, hill, or building in the view of the player eats valuable graphics memory and processing speed. With long vistas of buildings the number of objects multiplies and many games either fail to display them at distance, resulting in them popping up into view at the last minute,

or build intentionally short perspectives which lead to a claustrophobic feel. Using inspired and unique techniques, the team were able to show fabulous landscapes that stretch far into the distance. While wonderful for the game's realism, it creates a lot of work in terms of data collection. For example, the team working on the Grand Canyon had to survey and photograph 15 square miles (40 square kilometers) of territory.

Other achievements are evident in the fidelity of the real-time reflections, the subtle effects of smoke and dust particles, and the glare from direct sunlight. Less obvious but just as important to realism are the shadows that are sharp as you would expect from a clear midday sky, yet soften as clouds obscure the sun. The combined effect is so close to actual film that it becomes difficult to distinguish from the real thing.

FOR REAL-TIME 3D SPEED IS CRITICAL. THE GRAPHICS
ENGINE, WITH HELP FROM THE HARDWARE, HAS TO MAINTAIN
A HIGH FRAME RATE TO KEEP THE IMAGE MOVING SMOOTHLY.

1-4. These images show the replay function in action. The software governing the cameras automatically selects the best camera to cover the race in a contemporary, sports-reporting style.

5. Times Square, New York, in an uncharacteristically quiet moment. Look at the variety in the buildings that stretch into the distance—all accurately modeled on their counterparts in the real New York.

VISUAL EFFECTS
THE REALISM OF GT

086

THE GRAPHICS TEAM HAVE STUDIED THOUSANDS OF PHOTOS, VIDEOS, AND REAL RACES. THEY'VE PICKED THEM APART AT DIFFERENT VENUES ON DIFFERENT DAYS IN DIFFERENT LIGHT TO UNDERSTAND EVERY VISUAL NUANCE AND EFFECT. THEY THEN REBUILT THAT KNOWLEDGE, ADJUSTED, TWEAKED, AND POLISHED IT, AND ADDED THE ÉLAN ONLY GT CAN DELIVER.

GT4'S ATTENTION TO VISUAL DETAIL IS MORE THAN JUST EYE-CANDY; IT HELPS TO IMMERSE THE VIRTUAL DRIVER INTO AN EVER MORE REALISTIC RACING EXPERIENCE.

The Audi TT Abt DTM racing through the streets of Hong Kong. From the lens flare of the headlights to the brightly colored neon signs, the visual impact is simply breathtaking.

1

3

2

4

GRAPHICS HAVE ALWAYS PUT GRAN TURISMO IN THE LEAD.
KAZUNORI SEES THE IMAGERY AS PART OF THE WHOLE
EXPERIENCE—IT'S IMPERATIVE THAT IT MATCHES THE QUALITY
OF THE GAME'S OTHER ELEMENTS.

1. Snow bursting from under the speeding tires of a 1969 Nissan Bluebird 1600 SSS.

2. A TVR Tuscan Speed 6 at Nanzenji, Japan. Notice the way the color glows in the autumn leaves.

3. The BMW McLaren F1 GT making sparks fly. Another example of special effects generated as a result of player-driving and the physics of the car in its environment.

4. The glamor of Las Vegas is subtly enhanced by the use of a virtual starburst lens above the Chevelle™ SS™ 454 on the in-game camera.

At a technical level all visual effects are handled by the graphics engine, as that is responsible for building the picture the player sees. No matter how efficient the engine, however, it is the artists who truly create the illusion presented on screen. For the purpose of this page let's redefine the visual effects as all those subtle adjustments that only an artist can make.

Perhaps the most pervasive of the effects is dirt. Grubby detritus and grimy marks are a product of everyday life, particularly life on high-speed race tracks and circuits where pulverized tire rubber, exhaust fumes, and surface grit collect on even the most diligently polished bodywork. It is a function of the graphics engine that the cars' finish becomes duller the longer you play without visiting the car wash, where the glossy finish can be reinstated—but at a small cost.

Other effects are directly linked to the physics engine. Dust trails, snow flurries, and surface water sprays are a result of the environment coming into contact with the actions of the car. At times the effect is so marked that it obscures the view of chasing drivers to become a very real component of the gameplay itself.

All of these effects can be seen in other games but Gran Turismo never exaggerates them; instead the artists have blended them together to create an environment in which they appear natural and understated.

089

5

6

5. The TVR Cerbera Speed 6. A slow shutter speed in Photo Mode creates a light trail from the rear lights of the other cars.

6. The Renault Clio Sport V6 Phase 2. Notice the subtle sheen on the road surface. The effect is correctly calculated for all lights, not only the car's headlights.

05 BHP

PHOTO MODE

THE NEW REALITY

090

KAZUNORI LOVES CARS, AND HIS OTHER GREAT PASSION IS PHOTOGRAPHY. IN GT4'S PHOTO MODE HE BRINGS BOTH TOGETHER TO REALLY SHOW OFF THE AMAZING CAPACITY OF THE GT GRAPHICS ENGINE. PHOTO MODE IS A SIGNIFICANT STEP IN THAT IT USES THE GAME'S TECHNOLOGY TO EXPLORE A NEW FUNCTION BEYOND THE GAME ITSELF.

SUCH IS THE POWER OF PHOTO MODE THAT IT HAS THE POTENTIAL FOR GT TO APPEAL TO A WHOLE NEW AUDIENCE OF VEHICLE PHOTOGRAPHERS.

The TVR Cerbera Speed 12 at the Kokusai Forum in downtown Tokyo. The reflections of the building in the car's bodywork and the subtle light and shadow of the building itself are a car photographer's dream.

1. A Honda S2000 Type-2, at the Kokusai Forum, Tokyo, Japan. One of 60 additional locations where players can shoot the dream cars of their choice.

2. Not all GT's cars are modern high-powered sports models; racing cars such as this Mini Cooper simply adds to the fun.

3. A 1965 Shelby Cobra 427 s/c high up in the Italian Citta di Aria, Italy. Here the stylish sepia mode as been used. It's one of Photo Mode's many shooting set-ups.

4. A Mazda RX-8 sits in the beautifully tranquil gardens of Nanzenji, Japan.

5. The Mercedes SL55 AMG. Note the realistic slight sunray just touching the lens on the left.

6. A Mazda MX-5 at Nanzenji.

7. The Volkswagen Type-1 1100 Standard Beetle.

8. A 1969 Ford GT 40 screaming through the streets of New York. Using a slow shutter speed has blurred the car slightly, producing a sense of speed.

Photo Mode is new to Gran Turismo 4, and is an entirely new product in itself. The owner of GT4 now has access to the game's huge collection of cars and tracks, along with 60 further locations, and has the ability to photograph them with a sophisticated virtual camera. Players can now shoot their favorite supercar in a variety of exotic locations at will.

In addition, photographers can freeze the action during a race replay and set up their virtual camera, choose their lens, film type, filter, aperture size, and so on, and take a photograph. Various effects found in real photography also work, such as depth of field and motion blur, even evocative black and white. Photographers also have the option to use over 60 impressive fixed locations such as the Brooklyn Bridge and the beautiful gardens of Nanzenji in Japan to take their time setting up studio-quality compositions.

Because the data for the car, set and light information is held internally as 3D coordinates, the image is very compact and can be stored and emailed far more efficiently than in bitmap formats common to real digital photography. Most importantly, when the user goes to print his or her masterpiece, the image is generated at a one megapixel resolution, which provides a much higher print quality than is used on screen.

The results from Photo Mode are wonderful. With a single switch of focus on Gran Turismo, Kazunori has identified a completely new use for the valuable assets and digital environment Polyphony has created. It recasts the game as a whole new entity—a new interactive playground, where the races themselves are just one part of a much wider and more satisfying automotive experience.

093

9

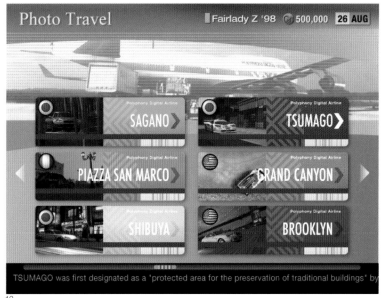

10

9. GT Photo Mode scene set-up. Camera and car are moved in both an overhead view and a lens view.

10. Selection screen for some of the 60 photo locations.

11. (Overleaf) The Toyota Celica GT-Four rally car passing the finish line on the Grand Canyon circuit.

PHOTO MODE IS EVERY AUTOMOTIVE PHOTOGRAPHER'S DREAM. YOU CAN CHOOSE FROM DOZENS AND DOZENS OF THE WORLD'S MOST EXOTIC CARS AND PHOTOGRAPH THEM IN EQUALLY EXOTIC LOCATIONS.

FAST CARS #5

BMW McLAREN F1

THE BMW McLAREN F1 GTR IS
THE FASTEST, MOST EXPENSIVE
AND POWERFUL PRODUCTION
CAR EVER PRODUCED.

096

VITAL STATISTICS: BMW McLAREN F1

MAX POWER:	627 bhp @ 7500 rpm	LENGTH:	4.92 m	ENGINE TYPE:	V12
MAX TORQUE:	651 Nm @ 5600 rpm	TOTAL WIDTH:	1.92 m	ASPIRATION TYPE:	Normal
DISPLACEMENT:	6064 cc	WHEEL BASE:	2.718 m	POWER/WEIGHT RATIO:	0.68 bhp/kg
WEIGHT:	915 kg	TREAD (FRONT):	1.598 m	TORQUE/WEIGHT RATIO:	0.71 Nm/kg
HEIGHT:	1.12 m	TREAD (REAR):	1.556 m	ARCADE MODE:	YES

The BMW McLaren was developed and built in Britain by a subsidiary of McLaren Formula 1 Ltd, with a specially designed engine from BMW. Initially 64 F1s were built in 1991 followed by an LM and a GT model. Eventually, in 1995, 28 GTR variants were released, bringing the total number of McLarens to just 100 cars when production ceased in May 1998.

The engine, a thundering 6.1 litre v12, was designed to give the driver a central position in the cockpit to provide equal weight distribution.

The F1 received a makeover in the GT version that extended the nose and modified the rear deck to produce a new, sleeker design, which could also hold the road better while minimizing drag.

The F1 GTR made its debut in the 1995 Le Mans 24-hour race and gained first place, with other F1 GTRs taking 3rd, 4th, 5th, and 13th places. To celebrate such an auspicious victory McLaren produced 5 special edition street-legal versions, the LMs, one for each GT that had finished the Le Mans.

A number of revisions and improvements were subsequently made to allow the GTR to meet BPR GT series race regulations, some of which resulted in 70% of the vehicles' components being replaced in the 1996 model. Further modifications were made in 1997, including a new sequential transmission, engine refinements, and a substantial weight reduction, again to meet new race regulations from the FIA GT and Le Mans 24-hour race.

06 BODY
CREATING THE CARS

098

GT4 CONTAINS AN INCREDIBLE 650 CARS FROM OVER 80 MANUFACTURERS, SPANNING THE PERIOD FROM 1886 TO 2005. KAZUNORI AND HIS TEAM HAVE CONCENTRATED ON HISTORICALLY SIGNIFICANT MODELS WHILE STILL INCLUDING RACE CARS RIGHT UP TO INTERNATIONAL RACING AND PRODUCTION CARS, SUPERCARS, AND A GOOD FEW CONCEPTS TOO.

OBJECTS, SUCH AS THE CARS IN GT AND ANY OTHER 3D GAME, ARE MADE OF AN INFINITELY THIN SHELL OF POLYGONS. THE FACT THAT THE ILLUSION WORKS IS DOWN TO A SENSE OF WEIGHT AND SOLIDITY CONVEYED THROUGH ANIMATION.

The Nissan Skyline GT-R on the Citta di Aria track in Assisi, Italy.

BODY 06

3D MODELING

100

2

4

3

5

2. Details of a Nissan Skyline GT-RV Spec II. Notice the level of modeled detail in the exhaust and tail fin.

3. The Dodge Viper GTS-R Team in Photo Mode at Brooklyn Bridge. Modeling artists always look at a car's distinctive overall shape first.

4. The Nissan Skyline GT-RV Spec II in close-up.

5. Racing older models is a key aspect of Gran Turismo.

As described in Chapter 05, BHP, the cars in Gran Turismo are constructed of individual points linked together by vertices and filled to create polygons. This mesh or wireframe is molded by the artist to make its distinctive shape. Model artists in the games industry have to work to certain restrictions on the number of polygons they can use for each object. Kazunori explains why there are polygon limits: "We have set rules that one car gets a limited amount of CPU (central processing unit) and GPU (graphic processing unit) costs. Therefore, cars that are complex in their appearance are more difficult to model." Cars in GT4 are around 3,000 polygons each, a tenfold increase from GT1 and GT2.

Modeling within these limitations is a skilled discipline; the artist has to carefully weigh different areas of the model with a number of polygons appropriate to both the shape and detail of that part of the model. Polygons are always three-sided and flat,

which is fine for buildings, but anything with curves requires a sufficient density of polygons to hide its angular nature. This makes cars, with their complex, often organic curves, both difficult to make and costly in polygons.

Where compound curves congregate around smaller details, the number of polygons climbs. Some of this detail can be artfully simplified, but a lot of it, such as the depressions around a faring or air intake, are important to the car's identity and have to be included if the car is to look like the real thing once it's in the game.

Many smaller details, such as the lines around doors and the hood, meshes in grilles, the lamps, and door handles are not modeled at all but reserved for the 2D texture map. Modeling such details is costly in polygons and time, and they're almost imperceptible as a 2D texture on the final model anyway.

1. The 2005 Nissan 350Z celebrates 35 years of this iconic sports car. The latest Z features a powerful 287 bhp engine and lightweight aluminum suspension.

"EXAMPLES OF SOME DIFFICULT CARS TO MODEL WOULD BE THE TOYOTA SUPRA AND THE HONDA (ACURA) INTEGRA. THE REASON BEING, THE MOULDING AND SURFACE IS SUBTLE AND ALSO SENSUOUSLY QUITE SIMILAR." KAZUNORI YAMAUCHI

THE MODELING PROCESS

102

"THERE IS NOT SPECIFICALLY ONE PART OF A CAR THAT IS DIFFICULT TO MODEL. THE MOST DIFFICULT PART IS TO MAKE SURE THE INTUITIVE FIRST REACTION UPON SEEING THE CAR IS 'LOOKS LIKE THE REAL THING', OR 'LOOKS COOL'. THIS DOES NOT NECESSARILY FALL IN LINE WITH THE ACCURACY OF MODELING EACH OF THE SMALL DETAILS." KAZUNORI YAMAUCHI

CARS ARE NOTORIOUSLY DIFFICULT TO GET RIGHT BECAUSE OF THE COMPLEX COMPOUND CURVES. SOME AREAS OF THE CAR, SUCH AS INTERIORS, CAN BE SIMPLIFIED, ALTHOUGH THIS IS OBVIOUSLY NOT POSSIBLE WITH CONVERTIBLES.

1. The 1973 Renault Alpine A110 1600S is a classic esthetic design. Its timeless curves are instantly recognizable for all the right reasons.

2. The Nissan Skyline GT-RV Spec II again. The model has to be accurate and work from every angle.

1

3

2

The artists begin the modeling process by surrounding themselves with photographs they've taken of the cars, images from other sources, and manufacturer's blueprints. The modelers then put together a profile view of the car from the front, side and top, which can be loaded into their 3D editing software as a guide. Cars in the game are built to real-world measurements inside the computer's virtual space to make sure everyone's models are the correct scale when they hit the track.

How the model is actually constructed is very much at the artist's discretion, and depends on how he or she prefers to work. Some will draw the car's profile in points, link them, and then extrude a basic 3D shape from that. Others will take basic building shapes known as primitives, such as cubes or spheres, and cut, or sub-divide them into more detailed shapes. Whichever method they choose the artists always work to get the largest overall shape correct before working on the detail.

In theory, Polyphony could directly extract 3D data from a car manufacturer's own models if absolute accuracy was the final goal, but Kazunori understands why an artist's eye is so important: "Sometimes replicating a car exactly may not necessarily give the viewer the impression that it looks like the real thing. Sometimes we need to modify or change things slightly (very slightly) to bring the image of the car closer to what the viewer recalls in the back of their minds."

1. The 2003 Mazda RX-8.

2. The 2002 Honda NSX-R Concept.

3. The Renault Avantime is an example of a model being worked on ahead of its real counterpart's market release.

105

4

5

6

7

8

4. A TVR Cerbera Speed 12. Interiors are slightly simplified but still look authentic through the transparent windscreen.

5. A race-modified BMW M3 GTR.

6. The retro charm of the Mini Cooper is faithfully reproduced in GT.

7. A Nissan Micra Acenta. Some detailed lines are modeled because the way they catch the light is essential to recognizing the model, as in the crease line along the edge of the windscreen.

8. An in-game detail from the Chrysler SSR pickup on the Las Vegas Drag.

THE 3D MODELS ARE CONSTRUCTED IN 3D MODELING AND RENDERING PROGRAMS. POLYPHONY'S ARTISTS USE ALL THE MAJOR COMMERCIAL PACKAGES.

SURFACING
THE DIGITAL REALITY

107

EACH CAR, ONCE MODELED, HAS A DETAILED PAINT JOB APPLIED IN THE FORM OF A PAINTED BITMAP IMAGE. IT INCLUDES NOT ONLY THE CAR'S GLOSSY FINISH BUT ALSO THE IMAGES OF THE WHEELS, HUBS, TIRES, GRILLES, CHROME, LICENSE PLATE, AND EVERY OTHER DETAIL.

A 1970 Chevelle SS 454 on the Las Vegas Drag. The various materials on a car respond differently to light and reflections.

WHENEVER THEY CAN THE TEAM STUDY THE PAINTWORK OF THE REAL CARS IN ORDER TO REPLICATE AS ACCURATELY AS POSSIBLE THE COLOR, DEPTH OF FINISH, REFLECTIVENESS AND OTHER PROPERTIES OF THE CAR'S PAINT.

Polyphony apply as much attention to detail regarding the paint finish on a car as they do to modeling it. When they collect photographs of the car they are not only seeking to match the exact paint color but also the nature of the painted surface itself. For example, modern cars use complex polymer varnishes to seal the surface, giving the paint a deep luster which is not so obvious on older cars where the pigment is more superficial.

The artists can adjust the amount of reflectivity and specularity (glinting from bright lights and the sun) to achieve just the right effect. These effects can vary across the car's surface by using another texture map superimposed over the color map. This map is also hand-painted but in grayscale. The graphics engine then uses the level of gray in any one area to apply that level of reflectivity or specularity.

The texture maps are initially built from photographs, cut and patched, using a flattened-out template of the car model wireframe as a template to help position them. They then need to be heavily modified by the artist by hand, both flat and with reference to the texture in place on the model. Some fine details, such as the door lines, are picked out individually with painted-on shadows and highlights to give the effect of superficial 3D modeling. All the time the artist is balancing all of these details and checking the image against photos of the real cars on different tracks and in varied conditions. Although they can match the colors exactly to the real paint finishes, they have to check it on screen and sometimes subtly adjust it to better suit the TV display.

Covering a 3D object like a car with a flat image is difficult. The artists use what is called UV-coordinate information that is held in the points that make up the 3D model in order to position the map accurately. It's not unlike using pins to attach a sheet of latex to a 3D object. Racing livery, with its graphic lines and text, needs special attention because any distortion would be immediately obvious.

108

1

2

3

LIKE POLYGONS, TEXTURES USE VALUABLE SYSTEM
RESOURCES, PARTICULARLY GRAPHICS MEMORY, AND
SIMILARLY HAVE LIMITS ON SIZE, WHICH WITH GT
REMAINS A CLOSELY GUARDED SECRET.

1. A superb rear view of the Subaru Impreza rally car on the Grand Canyon track.

2. A 2000 RUF 3400S. Notice the paint surface that gives a realistic metallic finish.

3. A 1993 Alfa Romeo DTM 155 V6 TI with a detailed racing livery.

4

5

6

4. The Mitsubishi Lancer Evolution IV rally car. The level of detail and clarity achieved in the texture is astonishing and beyond any previous versions of GT.

5. A Chrysler Crossfire. See how effective the metallic finish is in the bright lights of Las Vegas.

6. A 1971 Plymouth Cuda 440 Six Pack.

FAST CARS #6

IN 1967 MAZDA BEGAN SELLING
THE COSMO SPORT WITH ITS
REVOLUTIONARY ROTARY ENGINE.
THE TECHNOLOGY HAS NOW
CULMINATED IN THE RX-8 SPORTS.

110

VITAL STATISTICS: MAZDA RX-8

MAX POWER:	238 bhp @ 8500rpm	LENGTH:	4.43 m	ENGINE TYPE:	Dual Rotary
MAX TORQUE:	211 Nm @ 5500 rpm	TOTAL WIDTH:	1.78 m	ASPIRATION TYPE:	Normal
DISPLACEMENT:	654 cc (x -rotor)	WHEEL BASE:	2.7 m	POWER/WEIGHT RATIO:	N/A
WEIGHT:	1345 kg	TREAD (FRONT):	1.5 m	TORQUE/WEIGHT RATIO:	N/A
HEIGHT:	1.34 m	TREAD (REAR):	1.5 m	ARCADE MODE:	YES

The idea for Mazda's revolutionary rotary engine was first mooted by James Watt, and the first steam-driven design drawn up in 1846. Research on a petrol version was taken up in 1924 by Felix Wankel, who in 1959, with the help of NSU, completed the first working prototype. In 1963 Mazda, in cooperation with NSU, took over development toward a full production model, the Cosmo.

The engine is very different from the traditional piston configuration. It uses a triangular-shaped drive shaft that rotates in a circular combustion chamber with each edge of the triangle touching the sides to create three smaller chambers. Each of these acts as fuel in, combustion, and exhaust in turn.

The design requires far fewer parts, resulting in a lighter and more efficient design.

BODY 06

111

The RX-8 sees the latest iteration of the engine, Renesis, which is both light and responsive with the sound and feel of a hi-tech racing motorcycle.

07 CHICANE
BUILDING THE TRACKS

112

GT4 FEATURES OVER 50 RACE TRACKS WITH MANY FROM REAL-LIFE LOCATIONS, INCLUDING PARIS, HONG KONG, NEW YORK, THE GRAND CANYON, THE TSUKUBA CIRCUIT, AND THE NÜRBURGRING IN GERMANY. EACH TRACK IS A MASTERPIECE OF DIGITAL REPLICATION THAT MATCHES THE ORIGINAL IN BOTH VISUAL AND IN DRIVING TERMS.

THE CHOICE OF TRACKS WAS DEPENDENT ON A NUMBER OF FACTORS. SOME WERE POPULAR IN EARLIER VERSIONS OF THE GAME, OTHERS WERE INCLUDED FOR VARIETY. AND THEN THERE WAS THE TOUGHEST OF ALL—THE NÜRBURGRING.

A 2002 Renault Avantime in hot pursuit of a 2003 Peugeot 206 RC outside a wonderful rendering of L'Opéra, Paris, France.

1

2

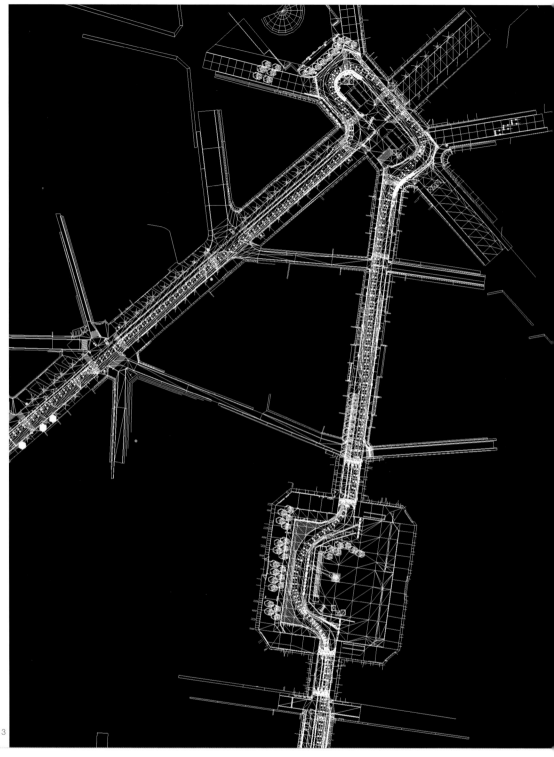

3

1. Kazunori on-site drawing diagrams of the track.

2. The Paris L'Opéra track recreated for the game.

3. The Paris L'Opéra circuit in wireframe form.
The attention to detail is quite staggering.

The tracks in Gran Turismo, like the cars, are created using a polygon mesh with a set of surface bitmaps providing the detail. Of course, compared to the cars, it's all on a much larger scale. The designers have to collate the 20-30,000 photos taken of each real track and match each location to its position using high-definition maps and on-site surveys.

The first task is to effectively lay out the track based on the maps, aerial photographs and height data from satellites. This early stage establishes the topographical shape of the track. For some, such as the New York circuit, this is fairly straightforward, as the track is relatively flat. Others are not so simple, among them Italy's Citta di Aria, which twists and turns up the hill on which the town is built, generating a mass of complex 3D shapes.

With the track surface in place, trackside structures and details can be added. After that the artists gradually add middle- to long-distance scenery or backgrounds. Scale and height need to be constantly checked. In terms of polygon density the tracks, like the cars, are subject to restrictions to take account of processor and storage limitations. Some structures, such as simple skyscrapers, however large, can be thrown up in a handful of polygons, while rocky landscapes need a reasonable minimum to appear acceptable. Generally, objects farther from the trackside can withstand less detail in the modeling.

Throughout the modeling process, textures are prepared from the thousands of photographs previously collected and stored. Where possible the textures are repeated as this saves precious memory on the PlayStation, although this technique is only used where it might be expected, such as repeats in architecture, or where it is unlikely to be noticed—on grassy hills, for example. As with the cars, whole areas of complex detail can be carried in the textures to avoid using polygons. Of particular note are the surfaces of the tracks themselves, which never contain repeat sections. Each metre of real track was painstakingly photographed to appear in the game, preserving all those scuff marks, drain covers, and fading lines for posterity.

Once all the elements are in place the overall visual balance is checked and fine-tuned. Once again, it rests on the skilled eyes of the artists to capture the "feel" of each track. Finally the trackside cameras are carefully positioned, as any TV sports channel would, to best capture the impending action.

115

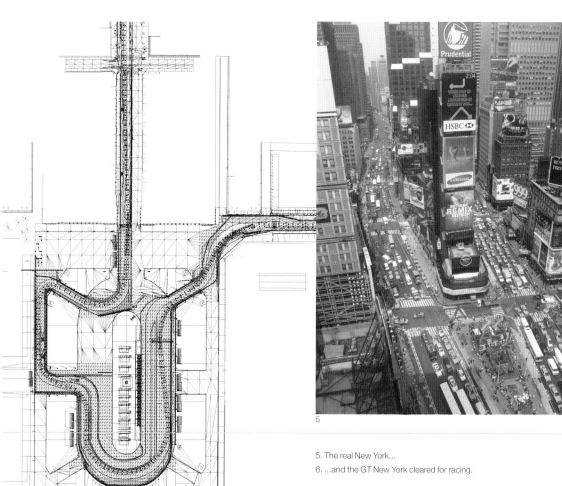

5

6

GRAN TURISMO 4 / ©SCEI

5. The real New York...
6. ...and the GT New York cleared for racing.

THE REAL TRACKS ARE MAJOR UNDERTAKINGS, WITH BETWEEN FOUR AND SIX DESIGNERS TAKING AROUND SIX MONTHS TO COMPLETE EACH ONE.

07 CHICANE

THE TRACKS

RECREATING THE GREATEST CIRCUITS IN THE WORLD

116

RACING IS AN INTERNATIONAL SPORT. DRIVERS ARE KNOWN FOR THEIR GLAMOROUS LIFESTYLES— JETTING FROM ONE FABULOUS LOCATION TO ANOTHER. GRAN TURISMO IS NO DIFFERENT. YOU ARE TRANSPORTED, IN THE FEW SECONDS IT TAKES TO LOAD THE DATA, TO THE STREETS OF NEW YORK, THE GIDDY HEIGHTS OF THE GRAND CANYON, OR THE TWISTING CHICANES OF TSUKUBA.

THE TEAM HAD TO LOOK TO A WIDE VARIETY OF TRACKS TO ENCOMPASS ALL THE RACING STYLES PRESENT IN GT—FROM A LEARNER'S SIMPLE OVAL, THROUGH CITY DRAG RACING AND OFF-ROAD RALLYING, TO THE ULTIMATE TEST, THE NÜRBURGRING.

Full throttle on the Las Vegas Drag. The tracks are as much about the atmosphere of the location as the challenge of the race.

1

2

3

4

1-2. The Dunlop arch on Japan's Tsukuba circuit. The GT version is at the top and the real one below it. All track measurements in GT4 are accurate to within 15 millimeters of the real thing.

3-4. The race control tower at the Laguna Raceway, California, this time with the real location at the top. You have to look closely to identify the real track—the giveaways are cleaner lines and a tidier skyline.

5

6

7

Kazunori and his team have a number of criteria when it comes to choosing tracks. The first is the overall balance between real and fantasy tracks. Kazunori explains: "Ideally I hoped to have a balance of 50/50, but this time (GT4) it looks like we will have more tracks based on real-life locations.

"In a fictitious track, we are able to adjust the number of corners, or change the composition and achieve the balance we are aiming for. This is obviously not possible with real-life tracks. This is why, as I mentioned earlier, the ideal balance would be a 50/50 split of real and fictitious tracks. Nürburgring was in fact a challenging track where we struggled with limited memory."

Real tracks are always high on the list of desires for players, and with good reason—everyone wants to try their luck against the big names in racing, and it's only on these tracks that you can compare your times with those of the professionals. If you follow the real races on TV you can enjoy the familiarity of knowing which corner's coming up; add to that the sheer thrill of virtually travelling the globe and visiting places you may never see in real life, let alone race on. For Polyphony they are fun, but expensive to produce because of the extensive data collection required.

Fictitious tracks have the advantage of control, which allows the team to carefully adjust their level of difficulty. With these tracks Polyphony find they can balance the difficulty curve perfectly, using them as bridges between real tracks.

5-6. Japan's Fuji circuit with the real track on the right. Detecting the real image here is almost impossible. The only difference is in the vegetation in the middle distance which appears neater because of repeat use of bushes.

7. A 2000 TVR Tuscan Speed 6 in Nazenji Park, one of the locations in Photo Mode. The locations were chosen with visual variety and esthetics in mind.

ALTHOUGH NOT QUITE ACHIEVING THE DESIRED 50/50 MIX OF REAL TRACKS AND FICTITIOUS ONES, THE BIAS TOWARD REAL TRACKS IS WHAT THE GAMING COMMUNITY WANTS.

07 CHICANE

With the keen eye of an artist, Kazunori was looking for visual variety and in GT4 he provides it in abundance. How different are the heady heights of Italy's Citta di Aria on a sunny afternoon from the Las Vegas Drag Strip at night, overhung with neon illumination? And how different a driving experience they provide: the drag strip tests your split-second gear changes, while in Italy it's all about focusing your line through tight corners.

Once completed, the team take a drive around their own virtual tracks with a video running next to them of a similar drive taken in the real world. The exercise is to compare and spot details that could be tweaked or enhanced. As these pages prove, it also serves as a testament to their incredible achievement in creating some of the most closely matched virtual scenery ever screened.

Of course the visual appearance of the maps tells only part of the story. Hidden in the code and invisible to the player is another map sitting on top of the color maps. It's the data map that tells the game engine how to treat surface area in play, from the slight drop in traction on a Paris cobbled street to the totally impassable concrete wall. Incline information is passed from the relative height of polygons to tell the physics engine to increase drag on steep uphill sections.

120

1

THESE SCREENSHOTS DEMONSTRATE HOW KAZUNORI HAS COMPLETED, ALMOST TO PERFECTION, THE TASK OF CREATING UTTERLY REALISTIC DRIVING ENVIRONMENTS.

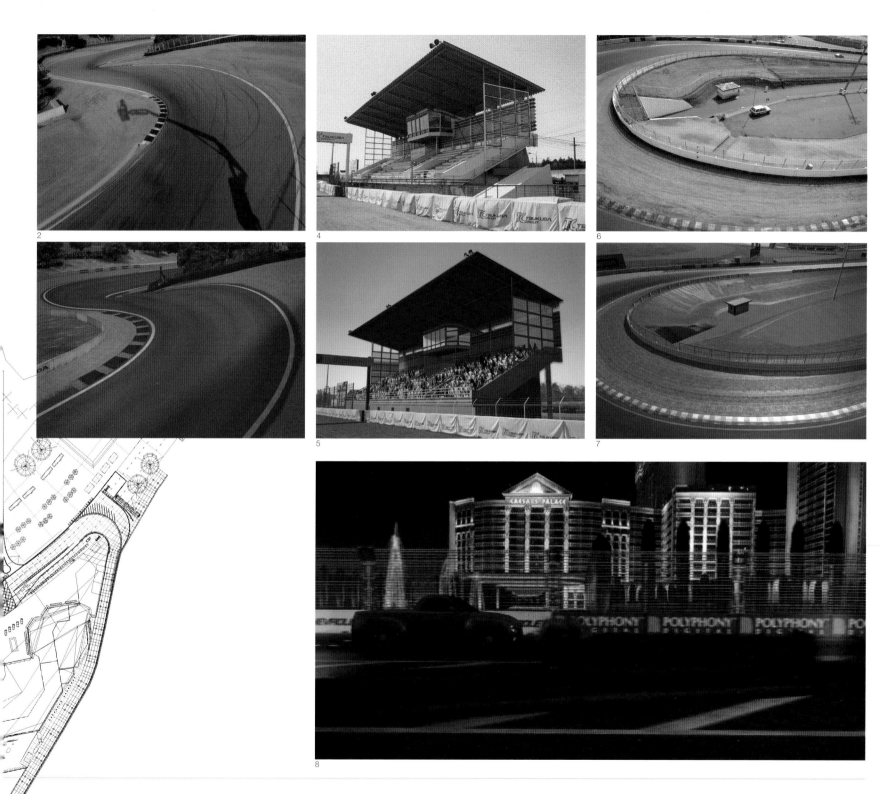

1. Citta di Aria (City in the Air), Assisi, Italy. Why go to the trouble of traveling to these locations in real life? With such realism, why not stay at home and become a GT tourist?

2-3. The real Tsukuba including a shadow of the photographer's crane, with GT's version below.

4-5. The stand at Tsukuba with GT's spectators waiting expectantly.

6-7. A spectacular bend on the Tsukuba circuit. GT's version shows some of the careful simplification applied by the artists where some grass textures are repeated, though it is barely detectable.

8. A 2003 Chevrolet SSR on the Las Vegas Drag Strip. The artists have captured the atmosphere, the very essence of the location.

NÜRBURGRING NORDSCHLEIFE
RECREATING THE WORLD'S MOST DEMANDING TEST TRACK

123

THE TOUGHEST TEST TRACK IN THE WORLD, AND THE TOUGHEST TRACK IN GT4 TO RECREATE. EVER SINCE THE FIRST GT IT WAS KAZUNORI'S AMBITION TO INCLUDE THE NÜRBURGRING CIRCUIT IN GERMANY, BUT ONLY WITH THE POWER OF PLAYSTATION 2 AND POLYPHONY'S NEW GAME ENGINE HAS IT BECOME TECHNICALLY POSSIBLE.

Putting a Nissan 350Z through its paces on the Nürburgring virtual track. An experienced test driver found he could experiment with different driving techniques that would be too dangerous on the real track.

AS A TEST TRACK, NÜRBURGRING CONTAINS ALMOST EVERY POSSIBLE VARIATION OF BEND, CAMBER, SLOPE, CURVE, AND INCLINE THAT A ROAD CAR IS LIKELY TO FACE ANYWHERE IN THE WORLD.

124

The team wanted the track to meet their stringent requirements for accuracy but collecting data was difficult, as it is in constant use by car manufacturers testing new designs to the limit. Every square yard of the 13-mile (20.8-km) track, and the surrounding landscape, had to be surveyed and photographed to produce the precise topographical data needed to reconstruct it digitally.

Nürburgring in GT is a testament to the incredible level of detail and realism achieved by Polyphony. With the track working in the game engine they decided to directly test it against the real thing. A test driver with 15 years' experience of Nürburgring drove a Nissan Skyline GT-R (R34) on both the real tarmac and in the virtual world of GT. The results were astounding. The lap time in the real car was 8 minutes 15 seconds. In GT4 the difference was just 5 seconds, only a 1 per cent variation between the two.

With this level of realism in mind the test driver returned to the virtual track and found he could experiment with different driving techniques that would be too dangerous on the real track. One such test was how a car will behave beyond its normal control limits. This has had a direct positive impact on car physics design in the real world, allowing manufacturers to test their prototypes in credible, but dangerous situations, and to modify designs accordingly.

For Kazunori, he has realized his dream of bringing the Nürburgring to GT. Now, with hundreds of virtual cars at his disposal he is interested, particularly with older models, to see how they fare among those tortuous bends.

THE TEAM'S PAINSTAKING DATA COLLECTION HAS RESULTED IN A VIRTUAL NÜRBURGRING THAT IS SO CLOSE TO THE ORIGINAL THAT TESTS MADE USING IT HAVE DIRECTLY IMPACTED ON THE DEVELOPMENT OF REAL CARS.

1. The 3D model, in wireframe view, of the entire track.
2. The Nürburgring as it appears in the game...
3. ...and the real thing.
4. Kazunori at a SCEE press event held at Nürburgring.

5

6

7

5. A composite wire-frame and rendered image of the Nürburgring circuit.

6. Data collection and collation.

7. Polyphony testing real cars on Nürburgring.

FAST CARS #7   NISSAN SKYLINE GTR

THE GT-R PUTS SUPERCAR PERFORMANCE UNDER THE HOOD OF A PUMPED-UP FAMILY SEDAN. IT IS THE ULTIMATE JAPANESE GRAN TURISMO.

126

VITAL STATISTICS: NISSAN SKYLINE GTR R34 V-SPEC

MAX POWER:	280 bhp @ 6800 rpm	LENGTH:	4.6 m	ENGINE TYPE:	In-line 6 cylinder
MAX TORQUE:	392 Nm @ 4400 rpm	TOTAL WIDTH:	1.785 m	ASPIRATION TYPE:	Turbo
DISPLACEMENT:	2568 cc	WHEEL BASE:	2.665 m	POWER/WEIGHT RATIO:	0.17 bhp/kg
WEIGHT:	1666 kg	TREAD (FRONT):	1.48 m	TORQUE/WEIGHT RATIO:	0.24 Nm/kg
HEIGHT:	1.36 m	TREAD (REAR):	1.49 m	ARCADE MODE:	YES

The first-generation Skyline was produced by Prince Motors in 1957 as a regular family coupé. The second-generation S50 gained recognition on Japanese race tracks in the 1960s, prompting the development of the 2000GT, which was designed to compete with Porsche.

In 1968 Nissan bought Prince and continued development of several generations of the Skyline. It was with the eighth generation, R-32, that the car won the status of supercar, using its massive 220 bhp to win every race it entered.

These images are of the Skyline R34 GT-R as it competed at the Nürburgring 24-hour race in 2004.

08 DRIVER
CHARACTERS AND AI

128

IT'S THE COMPETITION THAT MAKES THE RACE. DRIVER AI (ARTIFICIAL INTELLIGENCE) IS ALWAYS COMPLEX. WHEN RACING AGAINST THE COMPUTER, HUMAN PLAYERS ARE ULTRA-SENSITIVE TO THE WAY THEIR DIGITAL OPPONENTS BEHAVE, QUICKLY SPOTTING MECHANICALLY REPETITIVE MOVES OR UNFAIRLY TROUBLE-FREE DRIVING.

MAKING COMPUTER-CONTROLLED DRIVERS REALISTIC IS NOT THE WHOLE ANSWER. THEY ALSO NEED TO BE MATCHED TO THE SKILLS OF THE PLAYERS.

The 2003 Mazda RX-8 accelerating through downtown New York.

1

2

3

1. The 1992 Lancia Delta HF Integrale hill-climbing in the beautiful and historic Italian countryside.

2-3. The best interface with which to experience GT is a racing bucket chair and a good force feedback wheel and pedals. The Logitech Steering Wheel designed for GT4 has 900 degree rotation, the same two-and-a-half turning found in a real race-car steering wheel. The pictures show the Le Mans driver Soheil Ayari (far left) and Sebastien Bourdais, 2004 Champ Car World Champion (left).

PLAYER DRIVER
INTERFACE ERGONOMICS

How players interact with GT is divided into two areas: the first is the obvious driving interaction; the second, the selection's interface. As in most driving games, players are given a choice of view, from a trailing third-person aerial view to a first-person view in the cockpit, where your nose almost touches the track. The third-person view, though unrealistic in that it's clearly not the way a real car is driven, is popular because the player can enjoy watching their chosen car as it screeches around corners and roars up the straights.

The third-person view can cause frustration for beginners, however, because of spin-out on the straights. This happens when players attempt small corrections to the steering and, from the third-person view, the car appears to steer too harshly so they react with too much oversteer in the opposite direction. The problem repeats and before they know it they're facing the wrong direction. With GT4 Kazunori has corrected the problem by simulating real-car driving-assist technology.

The dashboard data is kept to a minimum with a semi-transparent speedo and rev counter. The maps are simple gray lines and apart from the position-counter, text is kept at its smallest readable size. The whole interface is designed to minimize interference with the player's experience of the race and as a result displays a svelte confidence common to the entire GT identity.

131

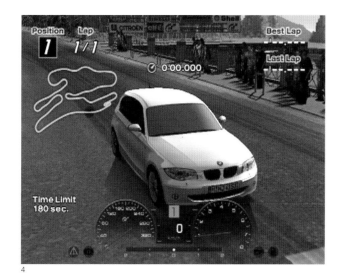

4–5. Examples of the driving interface. A third-person view (although this one is not a trailing view) of the 2004 BMW 1 Series in Costa di Amalfi.

THE FIRST-PERSON CAMERA IN MOST VIDEO GAMES TENDS TO USE A WIDER ANGLE THAN IS COMMON IN EITHER FILM OR TELEVISION BECAUSE PLAYERS NEED TO HAVE A BREADTH OF VIEW THAT REPLICATES HUMAN VISION.

08 DRIVER

ARTIFICIAL INTELLIGENCE

SMART SOFTWARE

132

ARTIFICIAL INTELLIGENCE HAS CONTINUOUSLY EVOLVED IN EACH VERSION OF GRAN TURISMO. ALTHOUGH A PLAYER'S COMPUTER OPPONENT IS NO MORE THAN A TANGLE OF PROGRAM CODE, DESIGNING IT REQUIRES AN UNDERSTANDING OF BOTH HUMAN MOTOR SKILLS AND PSYCHOLOGY.

POLYPHONY MEASURED THE PERFORMANCE OF PROFESSIONAL DRIVERS ON EACH TRACK TO BUILD A DATABASE OF TIMINGS FOR THE GT AI TO DRAW FROM.

1. A 1999 Peugeot 206 rally car cheered on by the crowds on the streets of Paris.

2. A 1992 Lancia Delta HF Integrale tearing through the ice. Being fully 3D, the spectators in GT4 are more realistic than in previous titles in the series.

1

2

3

1. A 1984 Mitsubishi Starion 4WD rally car streams past spectators at the Paris Rally. The addition of human figures is a welcome feature in the once-empty streets of GT.

2. The 1997 Mitsubishi Lancer Evolution IV rally car on the Grand Canyon circuit. Closed cars do not have drivers, which helps reduce the processing overheads. In future versions, however, Kazunori hopes to include drivers in all cars.

3. A 1995 Toyota Celica GT-Four rally car. Members of the crowd are now more animated in GT4, and can be seen dashing on to the track to take photographs.

4

135

Artificial intelligence in computer driving games is necessary to drive the computer-controlled cars in single-player games. Broadly, game AI can be divided into three areas. The first is ability, the second personality, and the last is the capacity to learn. Ability provides the computer-controlled player with enough basic intelligence to perform the task in question, for example doing a reasonable job of keeping the car on the road. Personality usually dictates the driving style and strategy; is the driver aggressively crashing through the pack in pursuit of the lead, or does he sneak through the inside of a corner to overtake? The ability to learn sometimes features in more complex story-based games such as RPGs but isn't a requirement for a satisfactory driving game.

Balancing these elements is complex because they are affected by intangibles such as personal taste and the real player's ability. Make AI drivers too good and the player can accuse the system of cheating and the desire to continue

playing drains away. Conversely, opponents who are too easily beaten reduce the challenge and risk the player completing the game in a single weekend. In GT, the AI is able to watch real-player drivers and make subtle adjustments to the ability of the computer drivers during the race while remaining within the parameters of their driving personality. This stimulates the digital driver either to try harder to catch up or drive less aggressively if in the lead.

Gran Turismo has to appeal to a very wide range of player abilities, with some highly experienced players trained up on the series expecting a really tough challenge. Kazunori also needed to set the limits realistically for each track. With the help of the fastest professional drivers on each track his team were able to match the AI drivers to within 0.3 seconds. Skilled players of GT now have the thrill of knowing that if they beat the very fastest AI drivers they are in the same league as some of the world's fastest professionals. That is some challenge!

4. The 2004 PlayStation Pescarolo C60 LMR Judd. Open top and convertible cars do have drivers. Kazunori's team, ever mindful of realism, have accurately modeled the physical movements of the body as a direct reaction to the car's movement. Now drivers are knocked around realistically by bumps in the road and turn their steering wheels to match the bends in the track.

POPULATING THE ENVIRONMENT WITH MORE REALISTIC HUMAN CHARACTERS WAS ONE OF KAZUNORI'S CENTRAL GOALS WITH GT4. IT'S TAKEN TIME THOUGH, AS HIS ARTISTS, WHO ARE MORE USED TO CREATING INANIMATE TRACKSIDE OBJECTS, BECAME COMFORTABLE WORKING WITH HUMAN FIGURES.

DRIVER

MULTIPLAYER
COMPETITION MODE

137

THE LATEST RELEASE OF GT IS
LAN (LOCAL AREA NETWORK)
ENABLED—A REVELATION FOR
THE SERIES. LAN PLAY IN ANY
GAME HAS A SIGNIFICANT
IMPACT ON THE WHOLE NOTION
OF VIDEO GAMING. THE FACT
THAT YOU ARE UP AGAINST
HUMAN OPPONENTS IS THE
MOST REALISTIC CHALLENGE
SHORT OF RACING FOR REAL.

The Honda NSX GT500 jostles among other racers on
the Tsukuba race track in Japan.

PERHAPS THE MOST ENJOYABLE ASPECT OF LAN PLAY IS
SOCIAL; SHOUTING TAUNTS AT EACH OTHER ACROSS THE
ROOM REALLY ADDS TO THE THRILL OF THE RACE.

138

1

Gran Turismo 4 allows up to six players to race against each other over a LAN (Local Area Network). Players bring their machines and TVs and hook them up using the PlayStation 2 network adapter so that they can all compete against each other on the same GT tracks. The effect is stunning, for although players have been used to split-screen multiplayer, it's a different class of competition altogether when you have the privacy of your own screen, not to mention the thrill of racing against more players.

In a stroke of genius Polyphony added the ability to hook up another couple of TVs to the LAN to act as race reporters through the use of the new TV Mode. The game can now generate two different live reports on the multiplayer action with the same realistic TV style of on-the-fly cuts and edits that GT replays are famed for.

Essentially enabling LAN allows for LAN parties, where groups of GT fans can get together and run serious competitions against each other. Over time, it is hoped that leagues will develop where the best players are put forward and eventually sponsored to compete at national and international levels. In time we will see the best GT players emerge to become international race drivers to rival the greatest professional drivers in the real world.

OF COURSE, THE MILLIONAIRE GT AFICIONADO WILL HAVE A
HALL FILLED WITH BIG-SCREEN DATA PROJECTORS, EACH
THROWING A LIFE-SIZE VIEW OF THE RACING ACTION.

1. A selection of Japanese GT touring cars on the Fuji circuit in Japan.

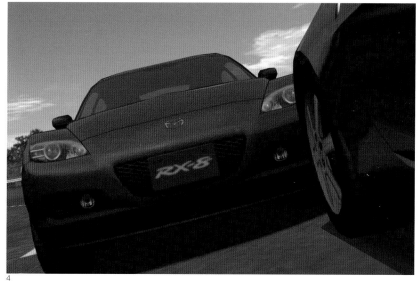

2. The Las Vegas Drag.

3. Regular stock cars, a VW Golf, an Alfa Romeo 147 GTA and a VW Polo on the Paris L'Opéra track.

4. A Mazda RX-8 in rapid pursuit.

5. A 1992 Lancia Delta HF Integrale tries to pass a Subaru Impreza. International LAN leagues may discover the next top race champions.

FAST CARS #8

WHEN IT FIRST APPEARED AT
THE 1970 TURIN MOTORSHOW,
NUCCIO BERTONE'S AMAZING
FUTURISTIC DESIGN STUNNED
THE WORLD.

140

VITAL STATISTICS: LANCIA STRATOS

MAX POWER:	190 bhp @ 7800 rpm	LENGTH:	3.7 m	ENGINE TYPE:	V6
MAX TORQUE:	275 Nm @ 6000 rpm	TOTAL WIDTH:	1.75 m	ASPIRATION TYPE:	Normal
DISPLACEMENT:	2418 cc	WHEEL BASE:	2.172 m	POWER/WEIGHT RATIO:	0.19 bhp/kg
WEIGHT:	980 kg	TREAD (FRONT):	1.432 m	TORQUE/WEIGHT RATIO:	0.28 Nm/kg
HEIGHT:	1.1 m	TREAD (REAR):	1.46 m	ARCADE MODE:	YES

The name Stratos derives from the word "stratosphere", evoking thoughts of interplanetary travel, appropriate for the car's spaceship-like dart shape. The Turin motorshow Stratos was a running concept prototype powered by a 1600 cc Lancia engine. The car captured the imagination of Cesare Fiorio, manager of the Lancia rally team, who conceived the idea of developing it into a purpose-built competition car. Rules at the time insisted that cars must come from a minimum production of 500 for a manufacturer to qualify, a process known as homologation. Lancia went ahead and Fiorio was given the opportunity to remodel the Stratos into his dream car. Bertone persuaded Lancia to fit a Ferrari Dino engine that had been marked for discontinuation and production finally began. From late 1974, when it first debuted, the Stratos dominated international rallying. Between 1974 and 1976 it won three consecutive World Rally Championship titles, including 50 European victories. In fact the car performed so well that other car manufacturers felt they could not possibly compete with the Stratos and withdrew from Group 5 rallying altogether.

09 TURBO
THE FINAL POLISH

142

IT'S A SPRINT TO THE FINISH.
PULLING A GAME LIKE GT
TOGETHER FOR RELEASE IS A
MAMMOTH TASK, WITH EVERYONE
WORKING ROUND THE CLOCK.
THE MYRIAD STRANDS ARE
WOVEN TOGETHER, TRACKS
LINKED WITH RACES, TWEAKS
MADE TO INTERFACES, PHYSICS
AND GRAPHICS ENGINES TUNED.
ALL IS TESTED, AND TESTED, AND
TESTED AGAIN.

THE LATEST VIDEO GAMES EASILY OUTSTRIP BIG HOLLYWOOD
MOVIES IN TERMS OF THE SHEER QUANTITY OF COMPLEX
ELEMENTS THAT HAVE TO WORK SMOOTHLY AS ONE.

The 1984 Mitsubishi Starion 4WD rally car,
photographed in Photo Mode and located in
the Kokusai Forum, downtown Tokyo.

1

1. The GT Mitsubishi Lancer Evolution IV rally car being
filmed and recorded going through its paces.

SOUND EFFECTS
CREATING THE TOTAL
DRIVING EXPERIENCE

THE SOUND OF THE CARS IS
CRITICAL TO GT. THE ENGINE NOTES
OF ALL THE CARS ARE RECORDED,
PROCESSED AND INTEGRATED INTO
THE GAME ENGINE. SUCH IS THE
PRECISION THAT A SHARP-EARED
DRIVER CAN EASILY IDENTIFY EACH
MAKE AND MODEL PURELY FROM
THE SOUND OF ITS ENGINE.

145

2

3

4

2. The 2003 Dodge SRT4. Environmental effects on the
car's engine sound were included, such as a change in
the tone when driving past hoardings and fences.

3. Even Doppler effects are reproduced in GT, with a car
engine sounding different as it approaches the camera,
whooshes past and drives away.

4. Recording the exhaust from a BMW.

GT SOUND EFFECTS ARE FAR MORE THAN JUST THE ENGINE
ROAR. WHEEL-SPIN, ENVIRONMENTAL EFFECTS,
DISTANCE, DIRECTION, SKIDS, GEARS UP AND DOWN, IDLE,
SURFACE NOISE, AND MORE ARE ALL FAITHFULLY RECORDED.

146

1

3

2

4

Sound completes the driving experience. As in a real car it gives important information to the driver, from setting revs at gear changes to signaling an engine stall. Far more important, though, is the excitement it adds to the drive. Deprived of the G-force sensation of accelerating in a real car, games rely on the sound of a screaming engine to deliver that visceral thrill.

The myriad sound effects that occur in GT4 are gathered during the early data-collection phase of production. Sound samples are taken from each car's engine and exhaust at several points—engine idle, revving to maximum revs, and at each gear change once on the road. The finer acoustic details, such as downshifting "pops" on meatier engines, are not forgotten. Again, like the huge number of photos collected, keeping track of data from the 650 cars requires detailed organization. The engine noises are then linked into the car's

physics engine so that when the player presses the accelerator the engine sound climbs in pitch and goes on to behave just as the real car does at key moments such as gear changes, during braking and at maximum revs.

External sounds are blended into the mix, including different tires rolling over varying surfaces. Racing across smooth asphalt on the Tsubaku circuit, for example, sounds very different from traversing the dirt tracks of the Grand Canyon.

Finally the sonic effects of each track's environment are taken into account. This is important because, just like visual effects, it contributes to the specific atmosphere of different locations. For example, when driving the open straights of Citta di Aria, the engine sound quickly dissipates into the clear blue sky; while racing the streets of New York, the sound echoes from the hard angles of the towering city blocks to create a louder, hard-edged roar.

INCIDENTAL SOUNDS ARE NOT FORGOTTEN, AND AS YOU'D
EXPECT FROM GT, MOST ARE SPECIFIC TO EACH TRACK—FROM
THE STARTING HORNS TO THE SQUEAL OF A CORNERING TIRE
TO THE CHEERS OF THE SPECTATORS IN THE STANDS.

1. Nothing beats the thrill of the ear-splitting roar of an unsilenced race engine. The Nissan R89C as driven at Le Mans in 1989.

2. A Peugeot 206 taking a sharp bend on the Paris circuit, complete with screeching tires and onlookers.

3. Modern cars such as this Audi have very different engine sounds, all of which are captured faithfully in GT.

4. The 1997 Mitsubishi Lancer Evolution IV rally car. Snow acts as a muffler and dampens the sound of the tires on the road.

5. Even the sounds of the crowd cheering on this 1995
Toyota Celica GT-4 rally car will have been carefully
emulated and programmed into the game.

MUSIC
MOOD CHANGING

148

1

There were two types of music in Gran Turismo: in-game menu music and tracks by selected artists for the player to enjoy while racing. With Sony Computer Entertainment being part of the Sony Corporation, Polyphony have access to many of the bands on the Sony label. The first game featured tracks by Ash, Cubanate and Garbage, while Gran Turismo 2 sported such names as The Foo Fighters, Beck and the Stone Temple Pilots.

GT3's opening sequence in the European version featured a special remix by Feeder. Some tracks were specifically written with GT in mind, such as Snoop Doggy Dogg's "Dogg's Turismo III", while others include "Kickstart My Heart" by Motley Crue and "Turbo Lover" by Judas Priest. The choices mainly reflect automotive themes, although some are more general, such as the Goldfinger cover of the song "99 Luftballoons" ("99 Red Balloons").

GT3 also saw the inclusion of a programmable jukebox so players could choose their music before rolling out onto the grid; an improvement from previous versions where only a single track would play. GT4 has a similar system called the Music Theater, which features a wider variety of styles by well-known artists from around the world, all of who have produced special remixes of their hit tracks exclusively for GT.

The menus use a general GT music track designed to keep the flow of action going while not interfering with the player concentrating on their selections.

Both the sound effects and music sound fantastic on the PlayStation 2 with a quality sound system able to handle Dolby sound and surround speakers.

THE MENUS HAVE A MUSIC TRACK THAT IS DESIGNED TO KEEP THE FLOW OF ACTION GOING WHILE NOT INTERFERING WITH THE PLAYERS CONCENTRATING ON THEIR SELECTIONS.

1. The wheels of steel. A member of the Polyphony team creating menu and other link music for GT4.

2. Peugeot 206. Driving and music: the greatest pleasures of life for many who play GT.

GAME TESTING

THE FINAL DETAILS

151

BUGS CAN BREAK A GAME.
ALL PROGRAMMING PROJECTS, AND
THAT INCLUDES GT4, UNDERGO
EXTENSIVE TESTING BOTH DURING
DEVELOPMENT AND PRIOR TO
RELEASE. IT IS
A GRUELING
PROCESS BUT
A VITAL PART
OF VIDEO GAME
CREATION.

An Alfa Romeo GTV 2.0 Twinspark. Its prowling stance
and good looks have made it a popular sportster
around the world.

POLYPHONY HAVE MANY PLAYSTATIONS SET UP AROUND THEIR
COMPLEX, RUNNING VERSIONS OF THE GAME. STAFF ARE
ENCOURAGED TO PLAY AND TEST AS MUCH AS POSSIBLE.

152

To say that game testing is a final detail is not strictly true, as the process is an integral part of a game's development from the very start. It begins at the simplest design level, while the team is discussing what should go into the game, what the new angle should be and what is and is not achievable. While Kazunori makes many of these decisions himself he also tests the ideas on colleagues, friends, motor-industry gurus, and sometimes players themselves.

The process of coding any software breaks down into a small percentage of time spent writing it and the rest testing it. At the most basic level, software coding is as simple as, "do this", or "do that", depending on certain other conditions. In a short routine of, say, five or six lines of code which together perform a simple algorithm, it is easy to predict the outcome. Start to multiply that by the many interconnecting links that rely on each other and things can easily go awry. For this reason programmers will write small fragments of code and test them both in isolation and when linked into larger routines. Modern methods of programming use the object-oriented approach which effectively places each task the code performs into single units. These are then easy to isolate from the rest of the code and test when problems arise.

Programming, particularly in a game as complex as GT, can throw up strange and unpredictable bugs. Those which crash the game are the easiest to deal with, because their catastrophic effect is clear. The toughest can have very subtle effects that are difficult to detect—such as a car veering very slightly to the left at 237.6 mph or the textures on a distant building being displayed upside down. Polyphony have to catch these bugs as they occur, to avoid delaying development and to retain the game's high quality.

Once the game reaches Alpha stage (a content-complete, pre-release working version) it is sent to Sony Entertainment for advanced testing. Like all games publishers, Sony Entertainment run teams of professional testers. Their task is to play the game for days on end; although it sounds like fun, they have to look for bugs and report them back to the developers for correcting. No game can be tested completely because of the almost infinite combinations of events. Some bugs will get through, but if the testers haven't spotted them they are considered too rare a set of coincidences ever to be encountered by players.

1

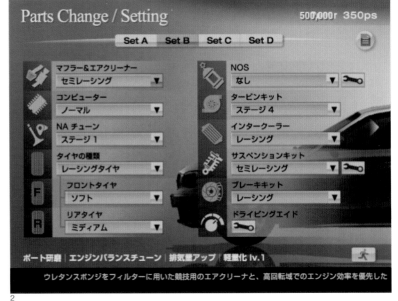

2

GAMES GO THROUGH THREE STAGES BEFORE COMPLETION:
ALPHA, IN WHICH ALL CONTENT IS INCLUDED; BETA, AT WHICH
POINT THE GAME CAN BE PLAYED; AND MASTER, THE FINAL,
BUG-FREE, COMMERCIAL VERSION.

1. Car selection screen. Each car has to be tested on every track that it can race on.

2. Parts selection. Every possible combination of parts and cars must be checked and tested.

3

5

4

6

3. A Mitsubishi Lancia Evolution attempting to hold its line on the ice.

4. A Subaru Impreza makes its way through another treacherous corner.

5. The 1973 Renault Alpine A110 1600S enjoys tearing up the streets of the Paris rally.

6. A Mitsubishi Lancia Evolution leaves the ground during a race on the grueling Grand Canyon track.

FAST CARS #9

IN 1991 THE MAZDA 787B WAS THE FIRST CAR POWERED BY AN UNCONVENTIONAL ENGINE TO WIN THE LE MANS 24-HOUR ENDURANCE RACE.

MAZDA 787B

154

VITAL STATISTICS: MAZDA 787B

MAX POWER:	700 bhp @ 9000 rpm	LENGTH:	4.782 m	ENGINE TYPE:	Rotary
MAX TORQUE:	608 Nm @ 6500 rpm	TOTAL WIDTH:	1.994 m	ASPIRATION TYPE:	Turbo
DISPLACEMENT:	1400 cc	WHEEL BASE:	2.662 m	POWER/WEIGHT RATIO:	0.84 bhp/kg
WEIGHT:	830 kg	TREAD (FRONT):	1.534 m	TORQUE/WEIGHT RATIO:	0.73 Nm/kg
HEIGHT:	1.003 m	TREAD (REAR):	1.662 m	ARCADE MODE:	YES

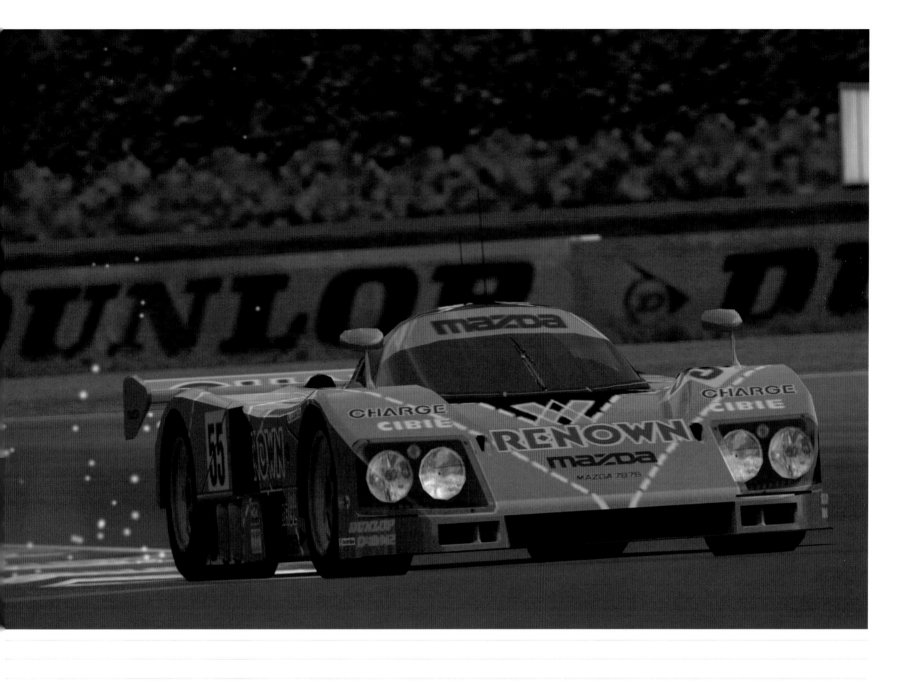

After competing at Le Mans for 18 years, the best result Mazda had achieved was seventh place in 1987 and 1989. Throughout this time Mazda had entered cars powered by their unusual rotary engine, which, although efficient and reliable, never secured a victory.

But in 1991 the team raced two new cars, the 787Bs, which differed from the earlier 787 (which remained their third car) in that they had a slightly longer wheelbase, narrower front track and modified suspension. All three cars had the same four-rotor engine.

The Mazda was running second, when, with just four hours left of the race, the leading Mercedes had to make a pitstop with mechanical problems. The Mazda's win not only marked the first victory for the rotary engine but was also the first ever win by a Japanese car at Le Mans.

10 WIN

BRINGING THE GAME TO THE PLAYERS

156

COMPUTER GAMES ARE BIG BUSINESS AND NOTHING IS BIGGER THAN A MAJOR GRAN TURISMO RELEASE. HOWEVER, COMPETITION IS FIERCE AND THE MARKETING TEAMS CAN'T REST ON THE LAURELS OF PREVIOUS SUCCESSES; THEY HAVE TO GET OUT THERE AND TELL THE WORLD THAT GT IS STILL THE KING OF RACERS.

AS GRAN TURISMO IS ALREADY THE BEST-SELLING PLAYSTATION GAME EVER, GT4 IS CERTAIN TO REPEAT THE SUCCESS OF THE PREVIOUS TITLES.

The 1995 Toyota Celica GT-Four rally car enjoying the testing Grand Canyon track.

1. The 1985 Renault 5 Maxi Turbo Group B rally car.

2. A Honda S2000 cutting through the neon nights.

3. A Subaru Impreza racing through the streets of New York.

4. A BMW enjoying the gloriously rendered scenery of the Citta di Aria, Assisi, Italy.

LOCALIZATION, MANUFACTURE AND DISTRIBUTION

159

Gran Turismo sells in over 100 countries and in nearly as many different languages. Traditionally the game is released first in its country of origin, Japan, with America and Europe following closely behind. The process of localization, which includes translation and possibly minor changes to suit local tastes, can delay the initial release into some territories. The decision to translate into different languages depends on the size of the market, with smaller countries having to make do with the European languages version.

Packaging design is handled at Polyphony with Kazunori himself using his experience in graphic design to have a direct input on the styling of the product. Many different variations on packaging are trialed before everyone agrees on the final version. The game's packaging is critical to its sales as it has to be distinctive on crowded shelves while still retaining the GT flair and assured quality. Although the packaging is not finalized until a few months before release, the logo design is settled upon much earlier during development. This is to give the project an identity to both the Polyphony team and car manufacturers during discussions involving using their cars. Along with the packaging, advertising material has to be designed, from point of sale display shelves to roadside hoardings.

Once the Beta version of the game has been thoroughly tested it goes to Master and the CD fabrication plants can roll into action. Actual manufacture time can be very short—just a matter of weeks—as the packaging and manual printing are finished in advance and are already waiting.

When finished the games are shipped to the retailer's central warehouses for distribution to individual shops. Timing is critical, for although the release date has slipped, once it is finalized hundreds of thousands of fans worldwide will be expecting to get the game on the day. Shops, both bricks and mortar and online, take delivery of the game a day or so before under strict agreement that they do not leak it in advance.

5

5. The 1989 Nissan R89C elegantly posed in Photo Mode at the Kokusai Forum, Tokyo.

SONY MANUFACTURES ITS PRODUCTS TO ORDER. HOWEVER FIVE MILLION UNITS ARE FORECAST FOR THE GT4 RELEASE, MAKING IT THE BIGGEST GAME SONY HAS EVER PUBLISHED.

10 WIN

MARKETING AND EVENTS

SPREADING THE WORD

160

WHEN A GAME AS BIG AS GRAN TURISMO 4 IS TO BE RELEASED, SONY ENTERTAINMENT REVS ITS GIANT MARKETING MACHINE TO LET THE WORLD KNOW ALL ABOUT IT. TELEVISION AND WEB ADVERTISING, TRACK HOARDINGS, SPONSORED RACE CARS, AND PRESENTATIONS ALL FUEL THE EXCITEMENT.

1

AS CREATOR AND POLYPHONY PRESIDENT, AND WITH HIS DETAILED KNOWLEDGE OF THE PRODUCT, KAZUNORI IS THE MAN BEST-SUITED TO MARKETING THE GAME.

1. Kazunori presenting GT4 to an expectant group of games journalists.

2. A Gran Turismo special day at the Nürburgring in Germany. Notice the GT-sponsored logos featured on the race cars.

Sony Entertainment's marketing muscle is evident in every corner of the world, with offices from Austrailia to Azerbijan and its flexing involves hundreds of staff. There are product managers in each major territory—Asia, USA and Europe—exclusively devoted to marketing the game. The relatively small number of leaders allows them to gather for strategy meetings every three months.

Although the pre-launch is the most important and busiest period for the marketing teams, work continues throughout the year. With game development cycles as long as three years it is important to keep the games, both previous iterations currently on sale such as GT3, and anticipated releases such as GT4, continuously in the gamer's radar.

There are a number of important events during the games industry's calendar, such as the E3 expo held in Los Angeles. Such events are where all the major companies unveil new products or build the expectation for previously announced games. At E3 2004, Sony devoted an entire room to Gran Turismo where journalists were invited to interview Kazunori and try out new features that had just made it into the game such as Photo Mode.

From time to time the marketing teams organize special events to promote GT to the press. An example was a trip to celebrate the inclusion of the Nürburgring track in GT held on the July 20th, 2004. Sony Entertainment flew 20 of the world's most respected games journalists to Germany to try their luck on the real track and GT's virtual track. The marketing team saw the event as a valuable opportunity to graphically demonstrate the incredible reality of driving the GT track compared with the real Nürburgring.

THE VIDEO GAME PRESS IS ALWAYS EAGER FOR NEWS OF GT, BUT OTHER AREAS ARE NOT FORGOTTEN, SUCH AS CAR PUBLICATIONS AND MAINSTREAM NEWSPAPERS AND TV.

1. An Audi TT-R 3.2 Quattro. Sony Entertainment arranged a number of Audi TTs, Honda Civic R-Types, 650 bhp RUFs and Alfa Romeos for journalists to trial on the Nürburgring circuit.
2. Driving the virtual Nürburgring.

3. Kazunori at a TV and press conference.
4. Advertising at the PlayStation-sponsored Pescarolo team pitstop.

5–6. A tire change for the PlayStation Pescarolo C60 at the 2004 Le Mans 24-hour endurance race. Note the GT logo on the rear-wheel arches.

THE LAUNCH
THE WAITING IS FINALLY OVER

165

AT LAST, GREEN. POLYPHONY'S EFFORTS ALL COME TO THIS SINGLE POINT IN TIME WHEN THE MOST EAGERLY AWAITED PLAYSTATION GAME FINALLY GOES ON SALE. THE RUN UP IS THE BUSIEST TIME FOR THE MANY MARKETING TEAMS AROUND THE WORLD.

A Pescarolo team race driver wearing PlayStation and GT logos at the Le Mans 24-hour endurance race.

VERY FEW GAMES COME OUT ON THEIR ORIGINAL RELEASE DATE. SLIPPAGE OCCURS BECAUSE OF THE UNPREDICTABLE NATURE OF SOFTWARE DEVELOPMENT.

Of course there is a great excitement as soon as a game like GT4 is announced; however the real push for the marketing teams begins in earnest six or seven months before the launch. A number of different strands have to be orchestrated to converge with the planned release. The promotional website has to be planned, written, and launched. TV commercials are written, storyboarded, shot, and edited while advertising is being planned for placement in magazines.

Details of the game are sent out to the world's media in the form of press releases, and a series of press conferences is booked. For Kazunori this is a very exciting but tiring time, as he is sent on a busy schedule of presentations and interviews, while at the same time steering the game through its critical final stages of development.

Releasing information to the press is a sensitive balance. If too little is released, incorrect and sometimes damaging rumors can propagate on bulletin boards. Give away too much too early and there is a very real risk that competitors will attempt to adjust their feature set to match GT. What's more giving away too much too soon could spoil the suspense for the fans.

The day of release. After three years of hard work the Polyphony team can finally relax in the knowledge that millions of happy gamers are, at that moment, glued to their TVs, completing the early stages of GT4.

166

1

3

2

4

AND KAZUNORI? HE TURNS HIS MIND TO GT5.

1. The GT logo, a muddied but resplendent badge.

2. An incredible ice sculpture of the GT4 logo at a special dinner held to promote the game.

3. The Pescarolo team's pit crew at the 2004 Le Mans 24-hour race.

4. Awards given to the GT series over the years.

5. Kazunori presenting Gran Turismo 4. He has to undergo a grueling round of press conferences to spread the word on GT4.

Circuit competitions such as the Lupo Cup are now held annually and are seen as an excellent low-cost starting place for budding amateur racers. Volkswagen's Lupo is seen as the way forward by the successful German company, by producing ultra-low-fuel consumption cars particularly for today's increasingly environmentally conscious markets around the world. Volkswagen scored a victory as the first manufacturer to break the 3-litre per 100 km barrier with the Lupo 3L. After testing the car, GT's test team

described it as an 'exciting ride with excellent, nippy, handling.' The Lupo first featured in GT3, and moves into top gear in GT4 to compete with the SEAT Arosa, BMW Mini, Ford Ka, and Fiat Cinquecento in the micro-car class.

GT4's Lupo contains all of the improvements found in the competition vehicle, including the punchy turbo-assisted 1.6-litre, 4-valve engine which serves up a maximum speed of 206 km/h (129 mph).

Polyphony captured all the fun of the Lupo's bright 'ice-cream' colors that make the range so distinctive on the track.

Direct all out speed is not the Lupo's forte. Instead the car makes use of its agility by maneuvering through packs of competitors confident that the excellent road holding won't result in a spin.

VW LUPO

MINI-CAR RACING IS A
CLASS THAT IS GROWING IN
POPULARITY—WITH A NUMBER
OF MANUFACTURES RELEASING
MORE POWERFUL GT VERSIONS
OF THEIR FUN 'CITY-CARS.'

VITAL STATISTICS: VW LUPO 1.4 SPORT

MAX POWER:	100 bhp @ 6,000 rpm	*LENGTH:*	3. 531m	*ENGINE TYPE:*	4cyl16V
MAX TORQUE:	126 Nm @ 4,400 rpm	*TOTAL WIDTH:*	1. 90 m	*ASPIRATION TYPE:*	Normal
DISPLACEMENT: 1390 cc		*WHEEL BASE:*	2.780 m	*POWER/WEIGHT RATIO:*	0.1 bhp/kg
WEIGHT:	1059 kg	*TREAD (FRONT):*	1.402 m	*TORQUE/WEIGHT RATIO:*	0.12 Nm/kg
HEIGHT:	1.448 m	*TREAD (REAR):*	1.388 m	*ARCADE MODE:*	YES

170

Kazunori aligns his sentiments with the romantic travelers who made grand tours of Europe in the 17th and 18th centuries in search of classical discovery. With Gran Turismo he is on a grand journey and learning along the way. Kazunori doesn't see GT4 as the end of the journey, despite its fabulous realism, rather a continuation of it.

The next stop will be the PlayStation 3. Kazunori is as full of anticipation as any other PlayStation player: 'Currently we face the lack of performance in every segment, therefore I hope that PS3 will improve performance in all areas 100 times more than what is available now.'

While all areas of GT4 could be improved, albeit in some cases by a few degrees only, Kazunori is keen to continue work on the human element of Gran Turismo. He is aware of the slightly barren nature of the driving environment, with a lack of drivers in most cars and rather wooden spectators, which is mainly down to limited resources on the PlayStation 2.

Perhaps the most desired feature for GT fans is the inclusion of collision damage to cars. For the time being Kazunori will not be drawn as to whether he will or not. However, you can be assured that if it does appear in GT5 it will be at a level of realism that surpasses anything that has gone before.

I asked Kazunori how he felt about being one of the stars of the game industry: 'Since day to day work on development keeps me so busy, I don't really feel like I am a star of the game industry. Our objective in this battlefield is to make quality products. Becoming famous does not help make our work easier.'

1

2

WHO IS THE BEST IN THE OFFICE AT GRAN TURISMO, AND IN WHAT CAR? 'THIS WOULD BE ME. I USUALLY USE THE HONDA S2000 OR THE NISSAN SKYLINE GT-R (R34).'
KAZUNORI YAMAUCHI

1. Kanzunori Yamuchi, President, Polyphony Digital.

2. Looking into the sunset on the virtual Laguna, GT4.

3. A 1997 TVR Cerbera Speed 6. The picture speaks for itself.

GLOSSARY

172

3D: In terms of video games and graphics it is images that are created from a mathematical 3-dimensional environment created in the game.

ABS(Anti-lock braking system): A driving assistance system in cars that limits the pressure to any wheel that decelerates too rapidly. This allows maximum stopping force to be applied, avoiding brake lockup which in turn causes skidding.

AI (Artificial Intelligence): The simulation of human intelligence by a computer. In games, AI refers specifically to the behavior of computer-controlled opponents, and how this affects gameplay.

Balance: In the context of gameplay, balance is a design goal, with the designer attempting to achieve a balance between the game being too easy and too difficult.

CGI (Computer Generated Imagery): An image created manually by an artist using various software packages and tools on a computer.

Code (Program code): The lines of instructions used to program a computer or console. Coding is the act of writing the code, also known as programming.

Development tools: Software programs used to create other computer based projects such as games. Many are, 'off the shelf', such as graphics and paint programs while some are built for a specific task by the developers themselves.

Doppler effect: The changing nature of a sound emitted from a moving object, such as a car, as it approaches the observer then moves away. Discovered in 1842 by Austrian Physicist and mathematician Christian Johann Doppler (1803–53), the effect is the result of sound waves compressing on the approach, causing a higher pitched tone, then stretching as the object moves away, resulting in a lower tone.

EBD (Electronic Brakeforce Distribution): A driving assistance system in cars that dynamically alters the braking distribution between the front and rear brakes.

ESP (Electronic Stability Program): A driving assistance system that detects when a driver is about to loose control of a car and intervenes to regain stability through the combined use of other driving support technologies such as ABS and TCS.

FMV (Full Motion Video): Short animation or movie sequences used in a game's introduction, at cut scenes during play, or for demonstration purposes.

Game engine: The overall program that runs the main part of a game. In the case of Gran Turismo it would be the driving part of the game, excluding the introduction, menus and selection screens. The physics and graphics engines are sub-systems of the game engine.

Gameplay: A loose term describing the mechanics of a game and the experience of the player as he plays it.

Graphics engine: The game subprogram that constructs the image and displays it on the screen as a series of frames in rapid succession (GT displays them at 60 frames per second). It handles calculating the 3D environment, lighting, textures, reflection and special effects.

Interface: The layer of screen icons, menus, and controller commands that allows the player to interact with the game.

Memory: In terms of computing it is properly called RAM (Random Access Memory). The area of a computer or console where data, such as the cars and track models and textures, and program code are temporarily held.

Multiplayer: A game in which more than one player participates at a time. Multiplayer games may be cooperative (the players work together to achieve a single goal) or competitive (the players battle for supremacy).

Pixel (Picture element): The individual cells of colour that a computer program builds into an image for display.

Polygons: The commonly used basic construction element of computer generated 3D environments that provide the 3-dimensional form of objects.

Physics engine: A system of in-game subprograms designed to simulate real-world physics within the game world. Objects move, tumble and fall according to the effects of momentum, weight, friction and gravity, adding to the realism and opening up new game mechanics.

Processor: Also known as the central processing unit (CPU). This is the hardware 'brain' at the center of any computer or games console. It is responsible for carrying out the instructions in the program.

Processor cycles: The fixed number of program instructions a processor can execute in a given time.

Graphics processor: A hardware component solely responsible for carrying out graphics instructions, from the graphics engine, and presenting them to screen.

Specularity: The effect of bright points of light on shiny surfaces reflecting from the sun or bright lights. The effect is usually created in games as a separate function of the graphics engine and graphics hardware.

Sprites: 2-dimensional graphic elements.

Textures and texture maps: The image that is wrapped onto the surface of a 3D computer generated-object to give it color and surface detail.

TCS (Traction Control System): A driving assistance system that helps to prevent loss of traction during acceleration by increasing the braking pressure on a wheel if it starts to slip, thus maximizing contact between the tyres and the road.

Torque curve: The trade off between torque, the rotation force from an engine, and speed generated while accelerating forward in a straight line. Every car engine generates it's own specific torque curve. At the bottom of the curve the speed is very slow while at the top the engine stalls with the maximum efficiency at the center of the curve.

UV: Also described as UV mapping. The co-ordinate system used to fit a 2D image onto a 3D computer-generated object. The UV map gives fixed points on the surface of the model to assign to points on the 2D image. The effect is similar to pinning a rubber sheet at multiple points to a 3D object.

Virtual: In terms of computing it refers to a world or environment constructed within the computer which can be a simulation of the real world or fictional.

Wireframe: A view used during game development of a 3D computer generated model that displaying it's underlying polygon structure as interconnecting lines. Sometimes also referred to as a mesh.

INDEX

174

ACKNOWLEDGMENTS

176

Thanks to all those who gave their valuable time to assist
the making of this book; with special thanks to:

Everyone at Polyphony Digital Inc.

At Sony Computer Entertainment
Jason Fitzgerald
Susan Nourai
Mark Valledor
Simon Roberts
Taku Imasaki

My brother, Dan Teubert, a GT fan.

Copyright
Page 12 & 13. Images 1, 2 and 4 are the exclusive copyright of Atari Inc.
Page 13. Image 3 is copyright Vectorbeam Inc.